I0482388

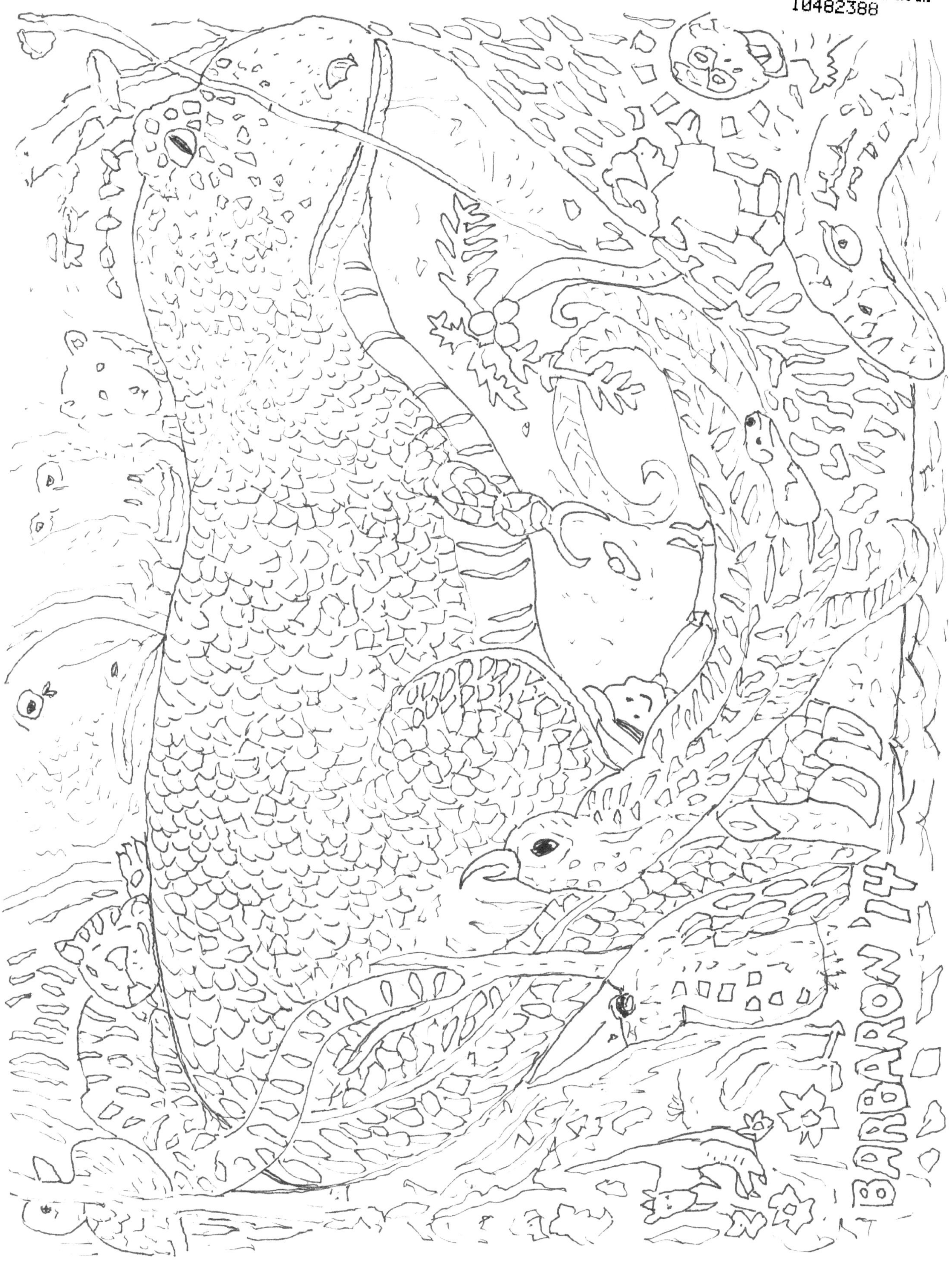

BARBARON #1 NOVABARO

TREE REX

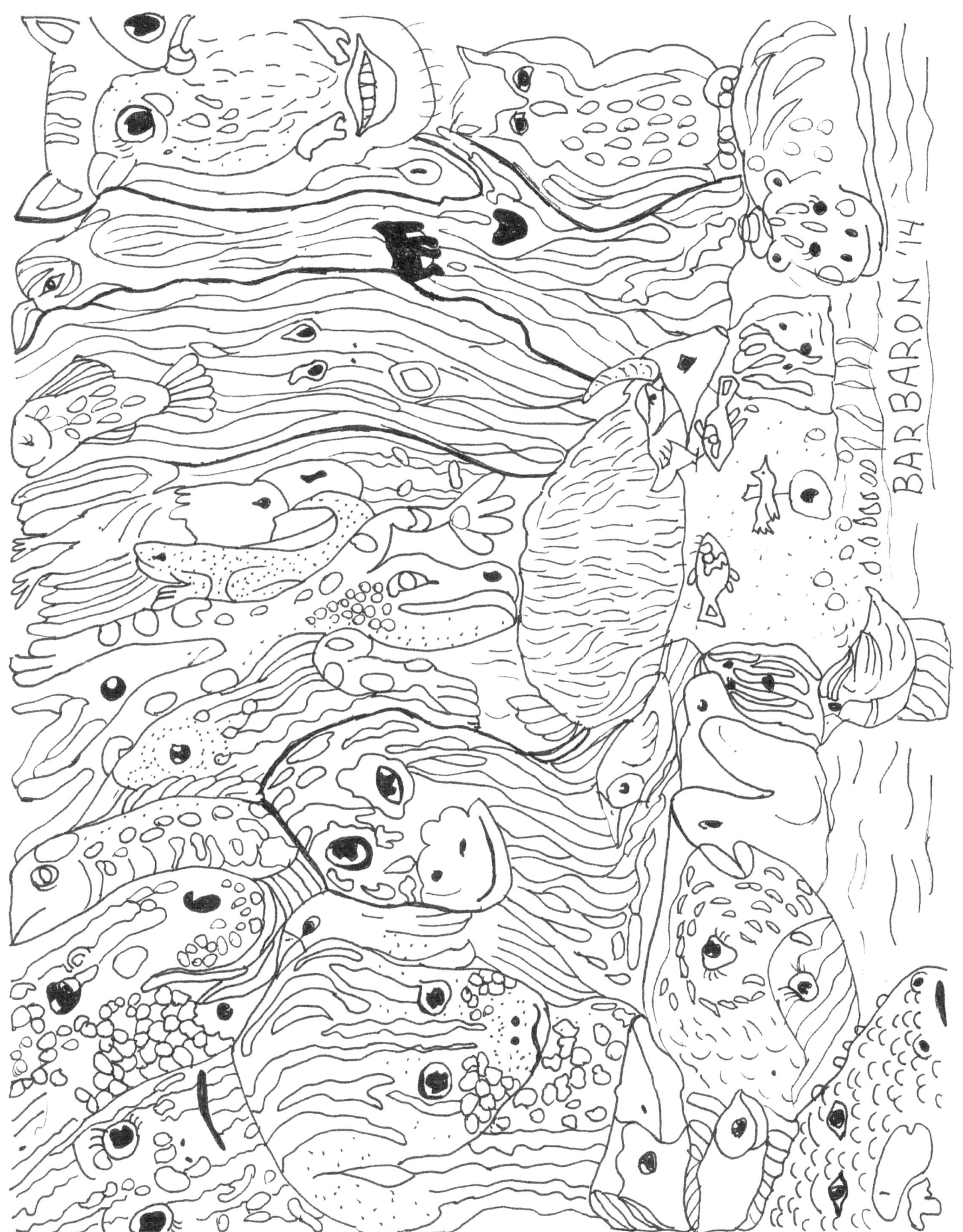

FOREST BLUES

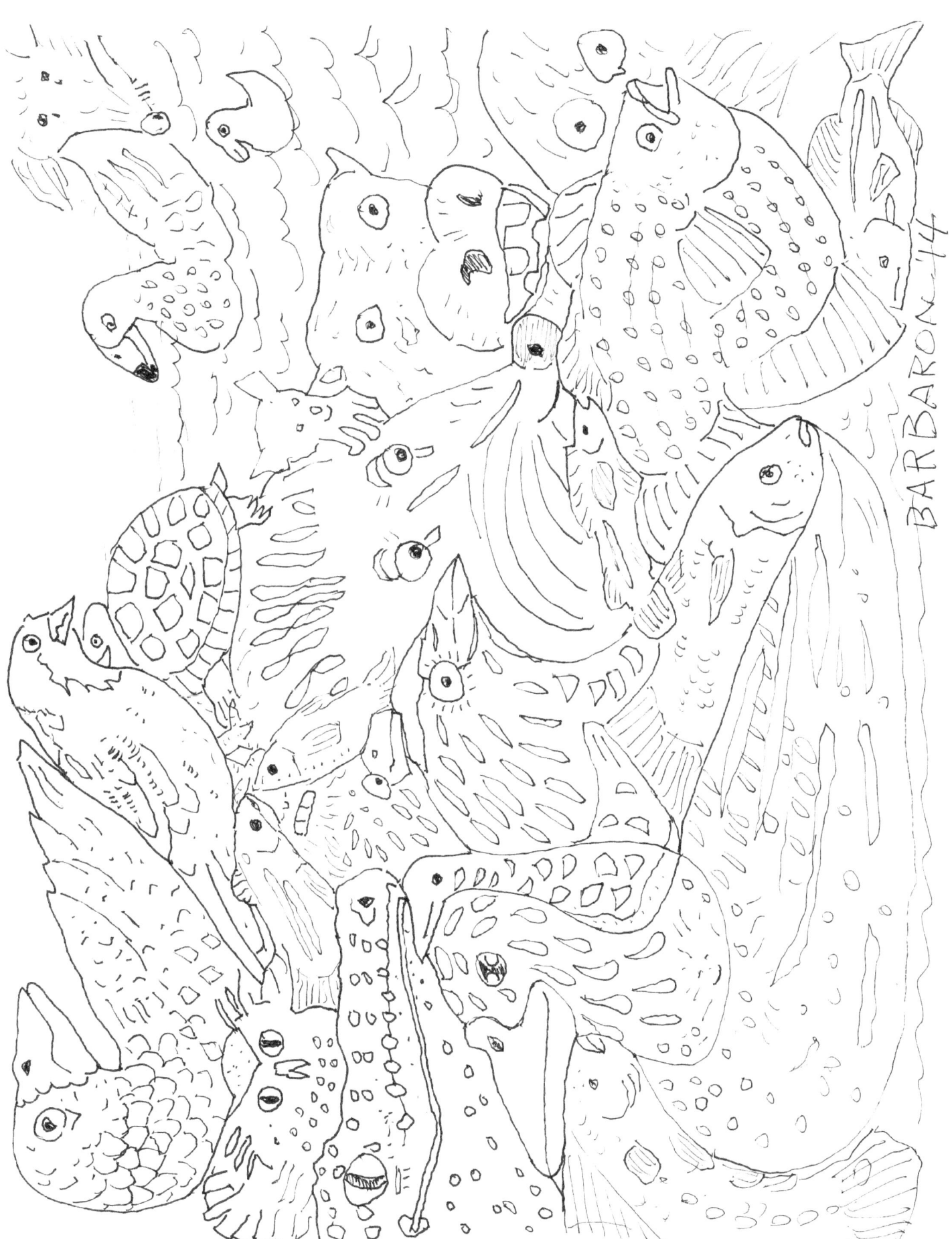

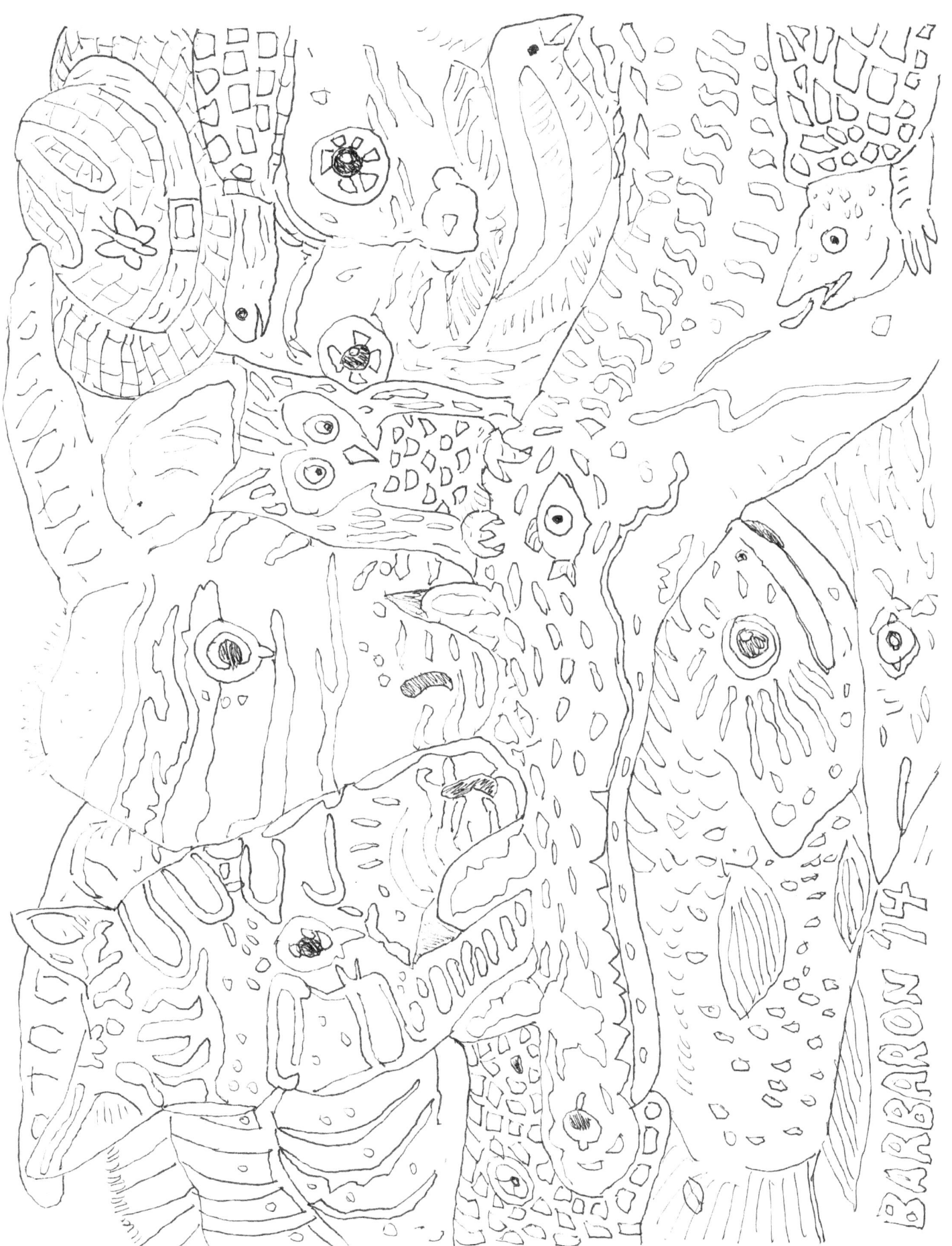

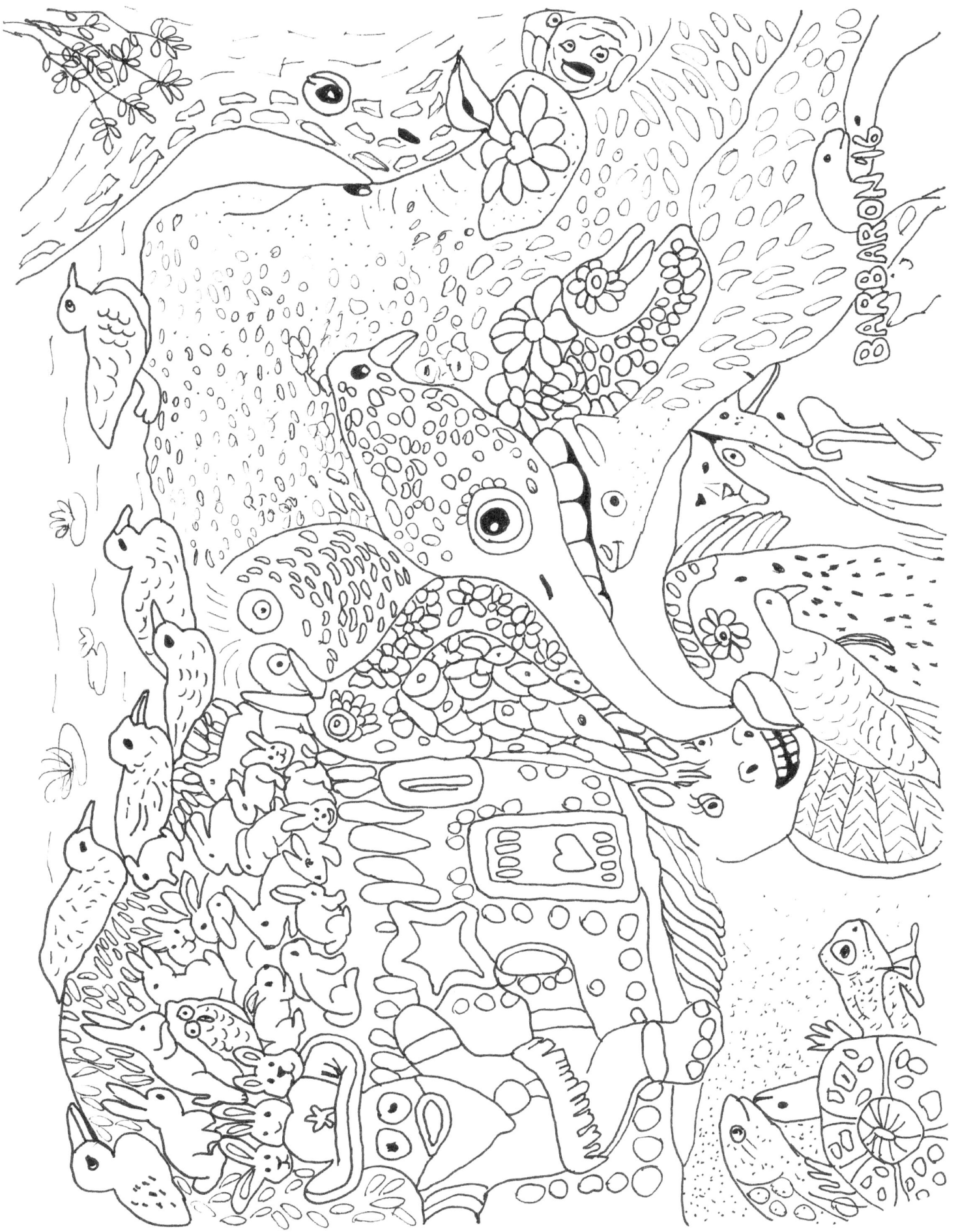

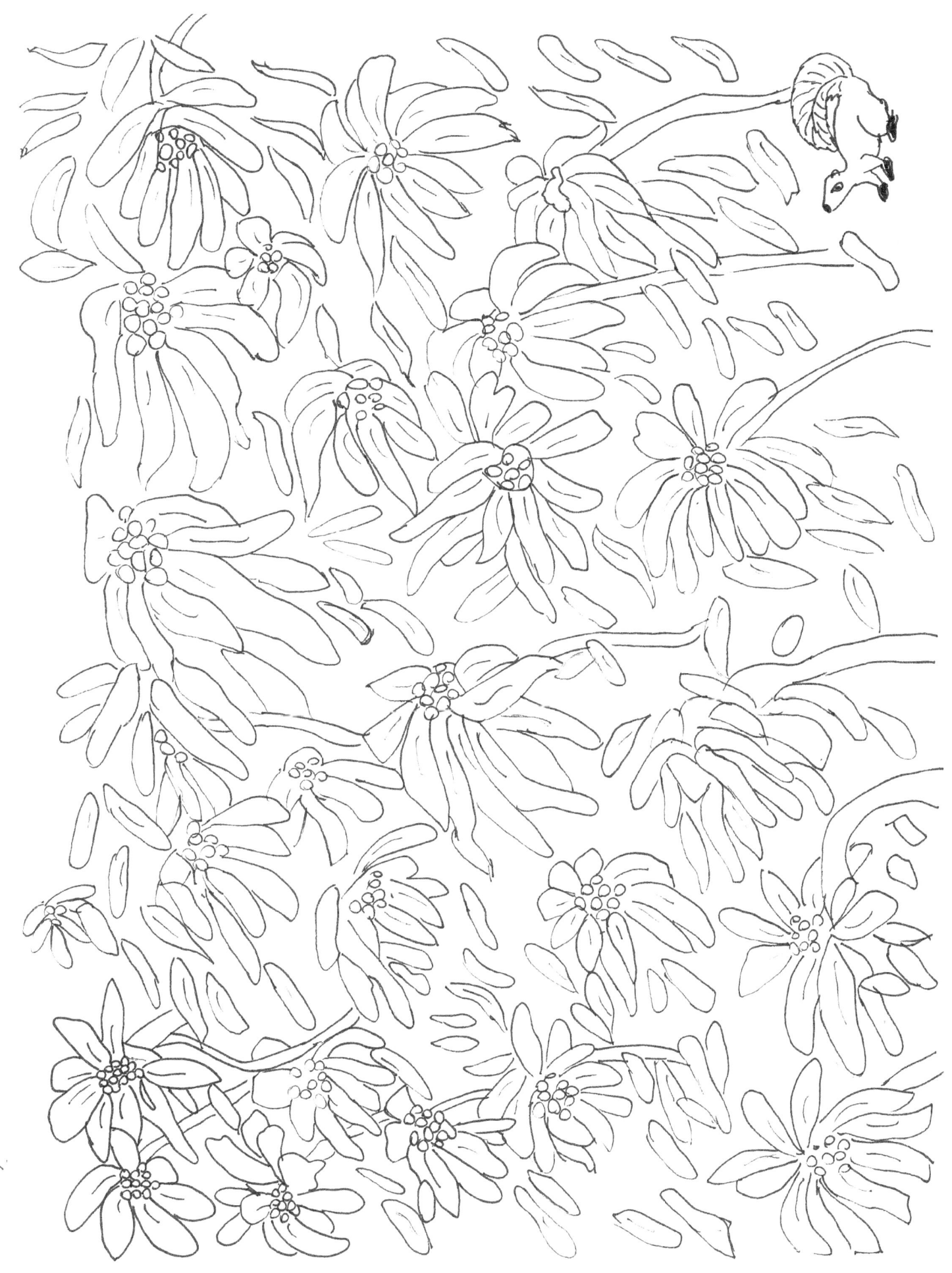

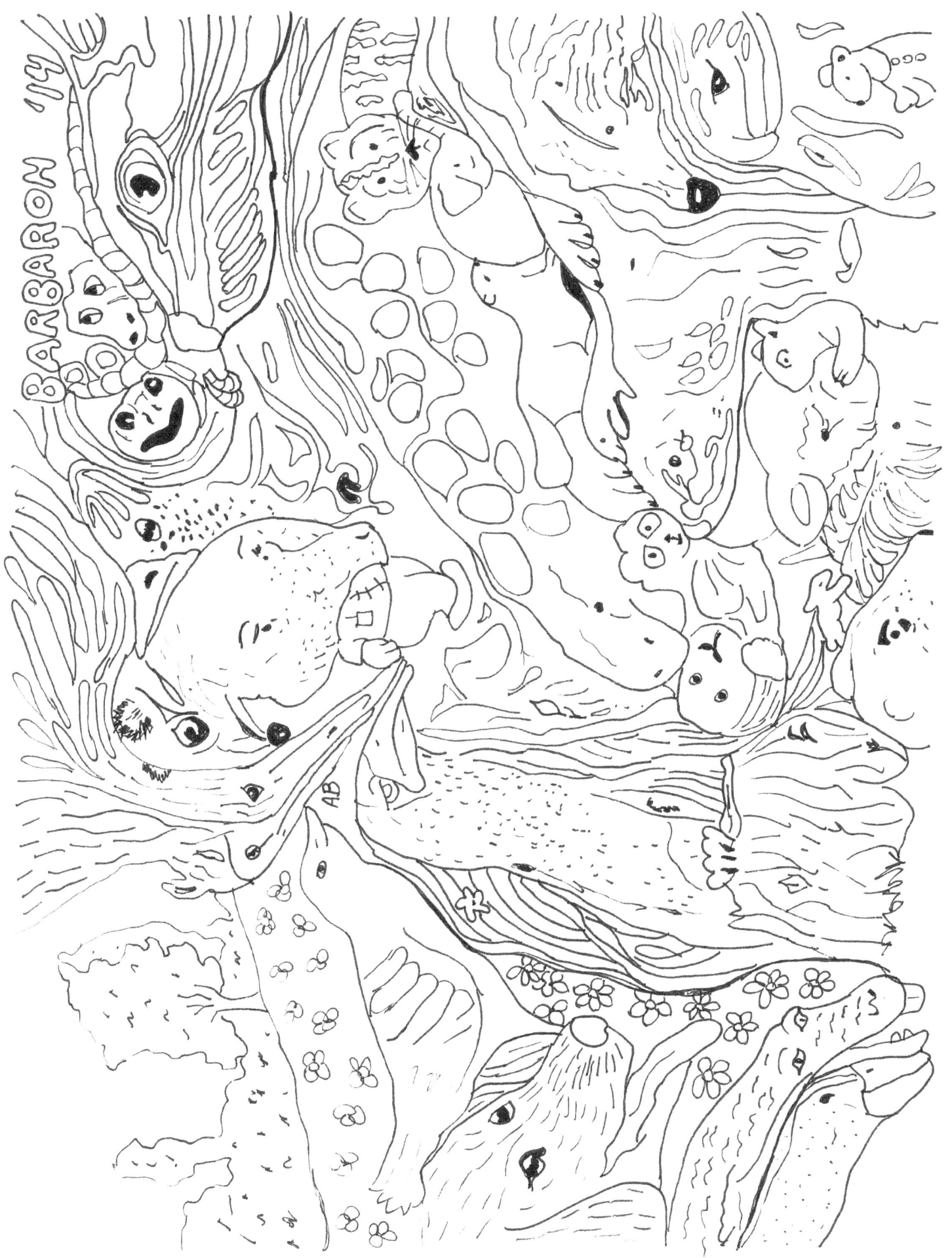

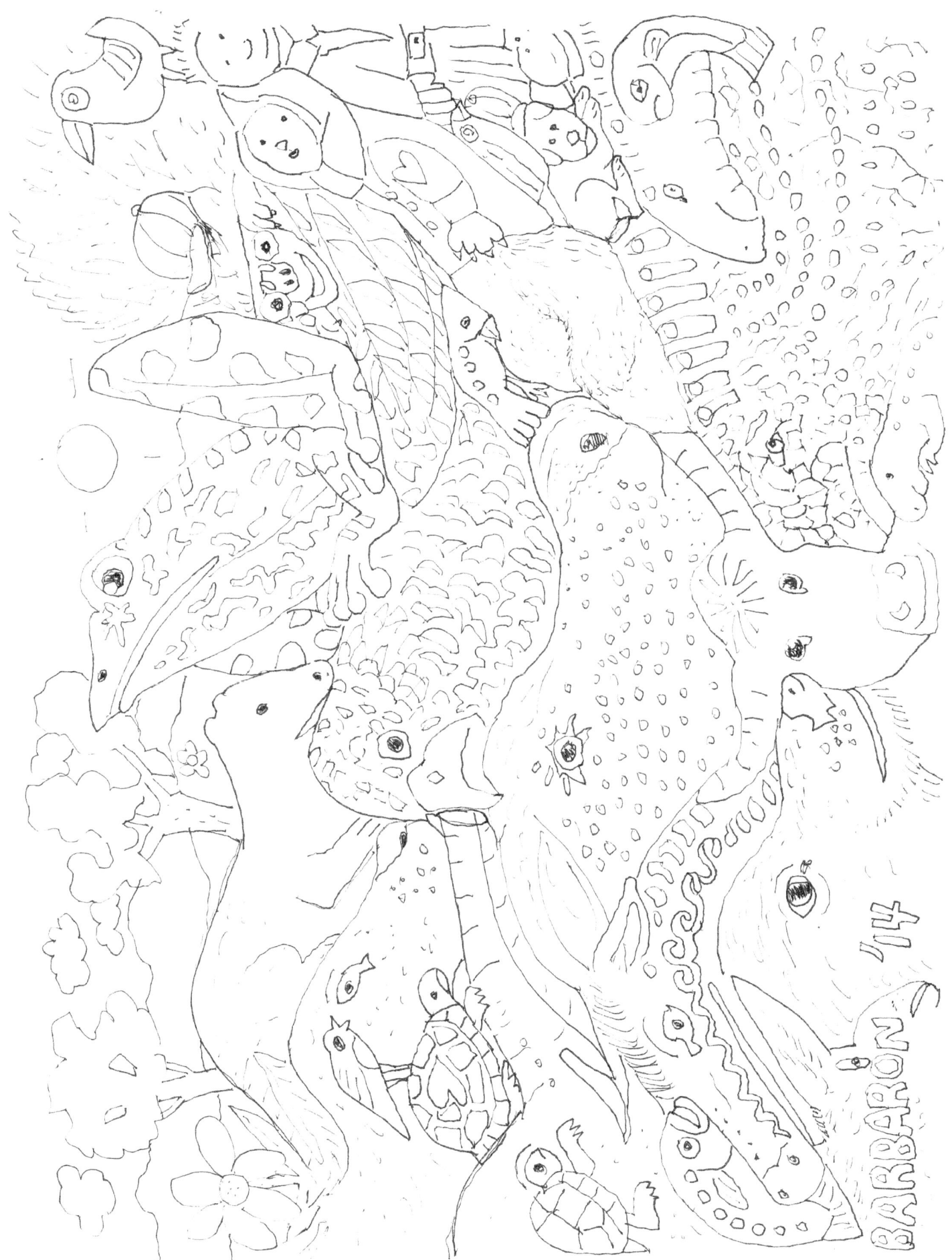

LITTLE RED RIDING FOX

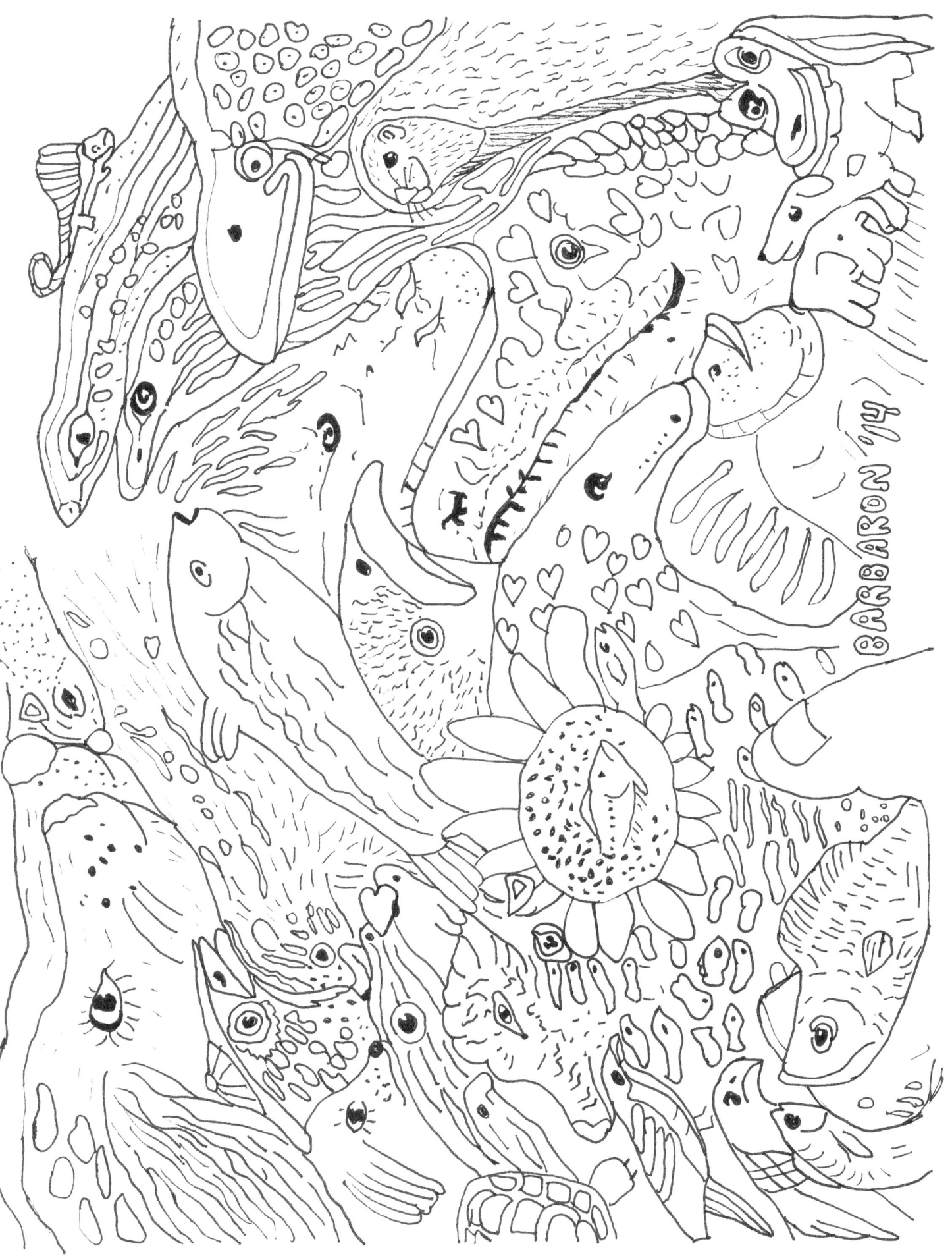

FISH IN THE HAND

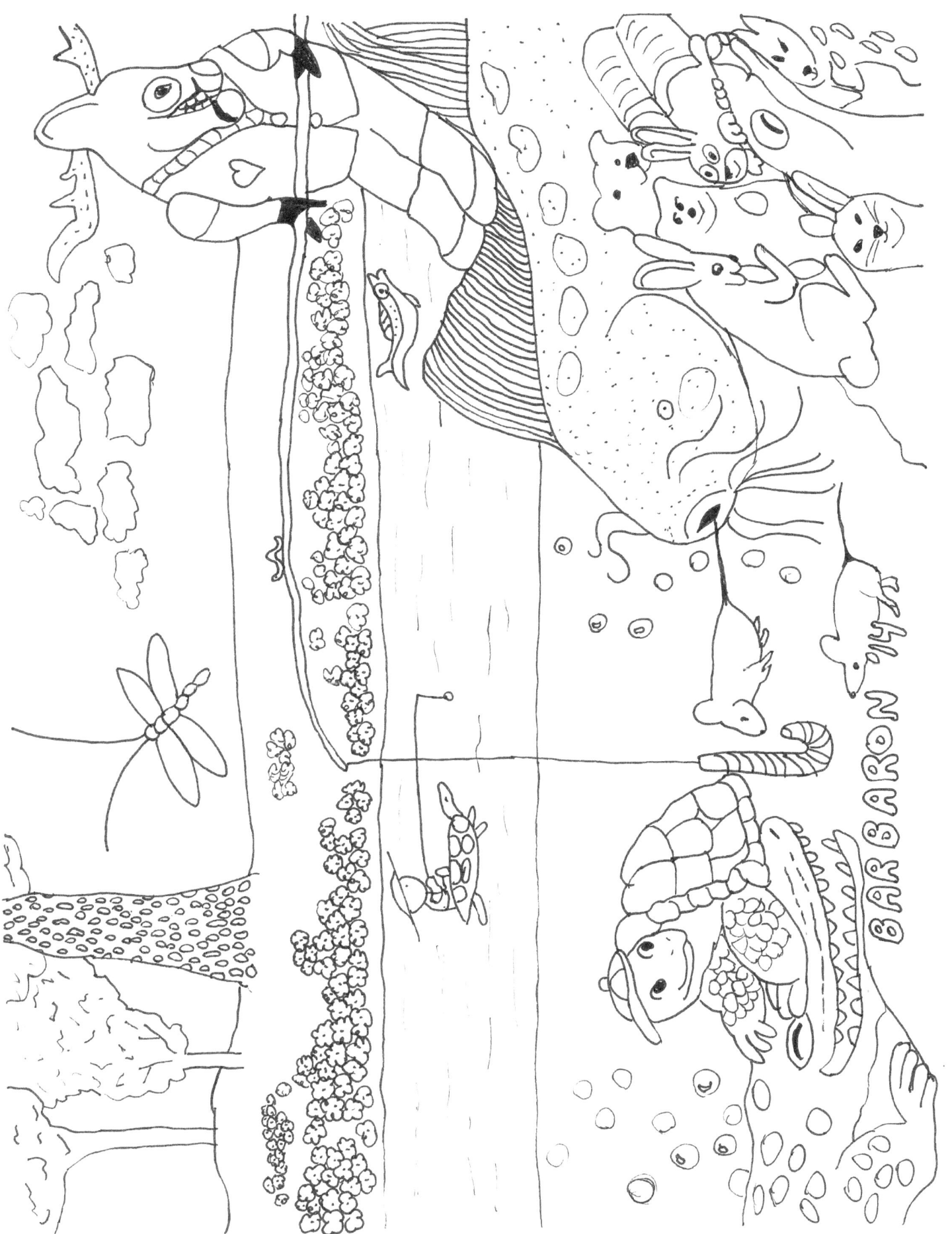

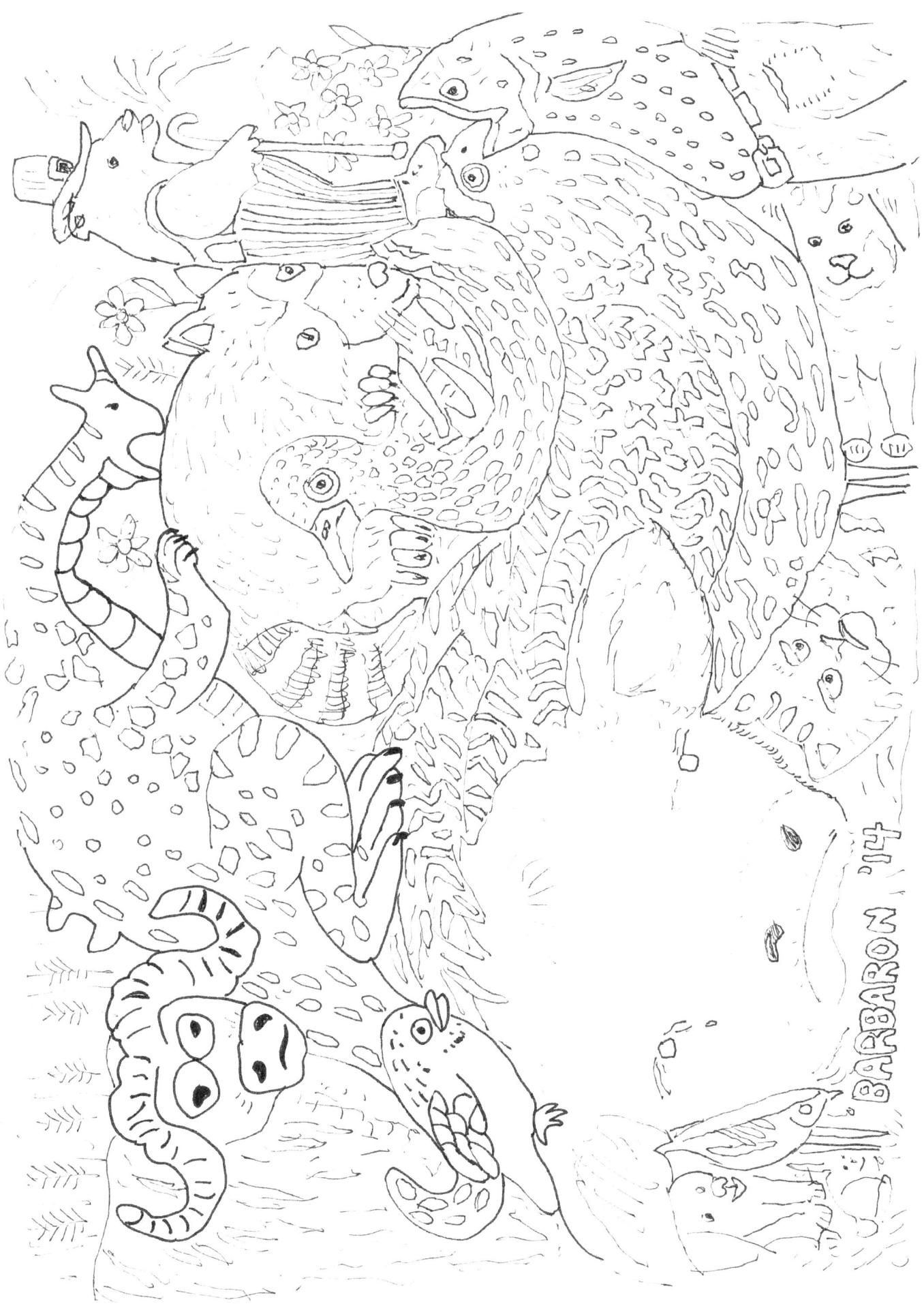

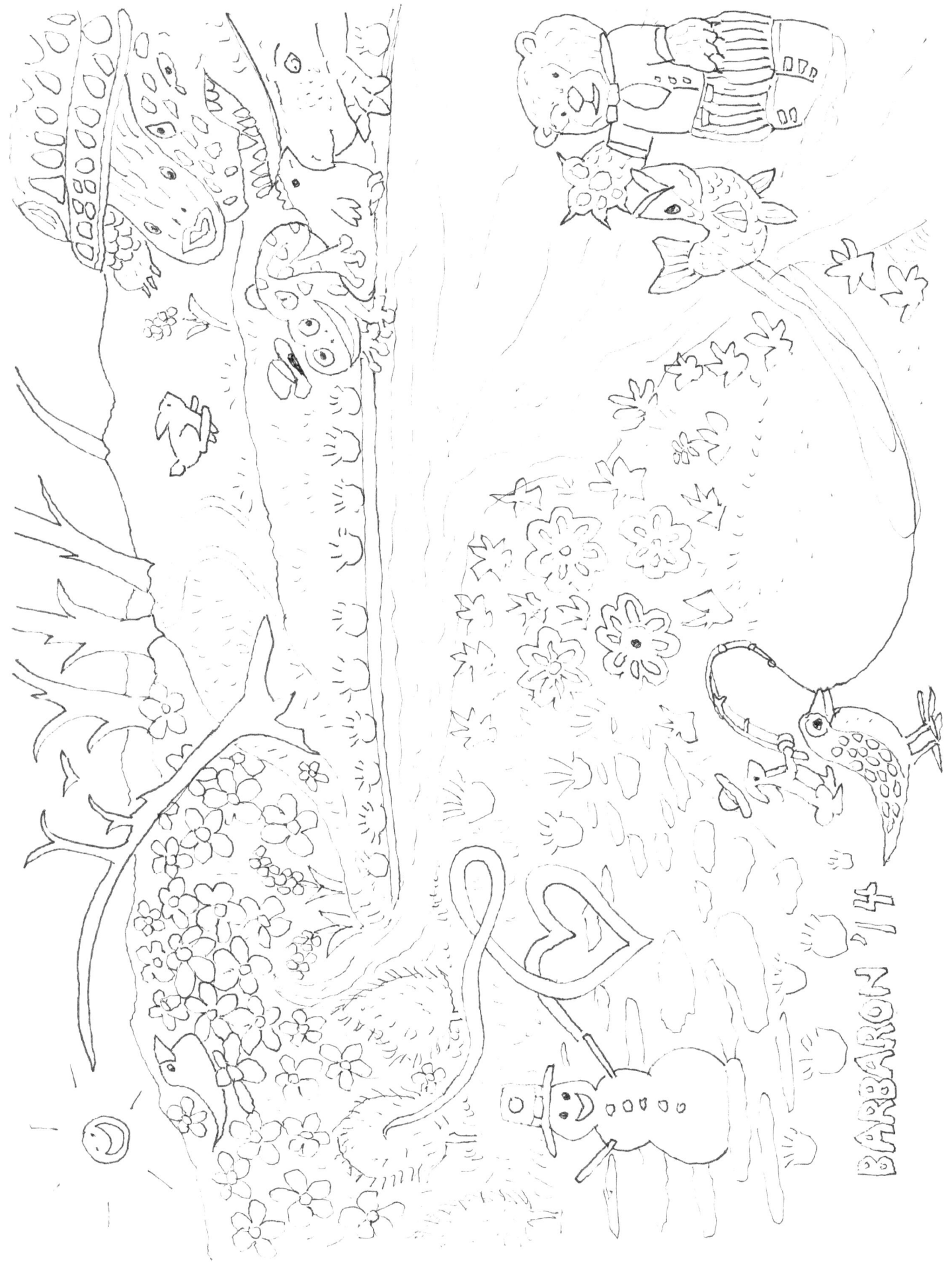

BARBARON ?/14

ONCE IN A BLUE SUN

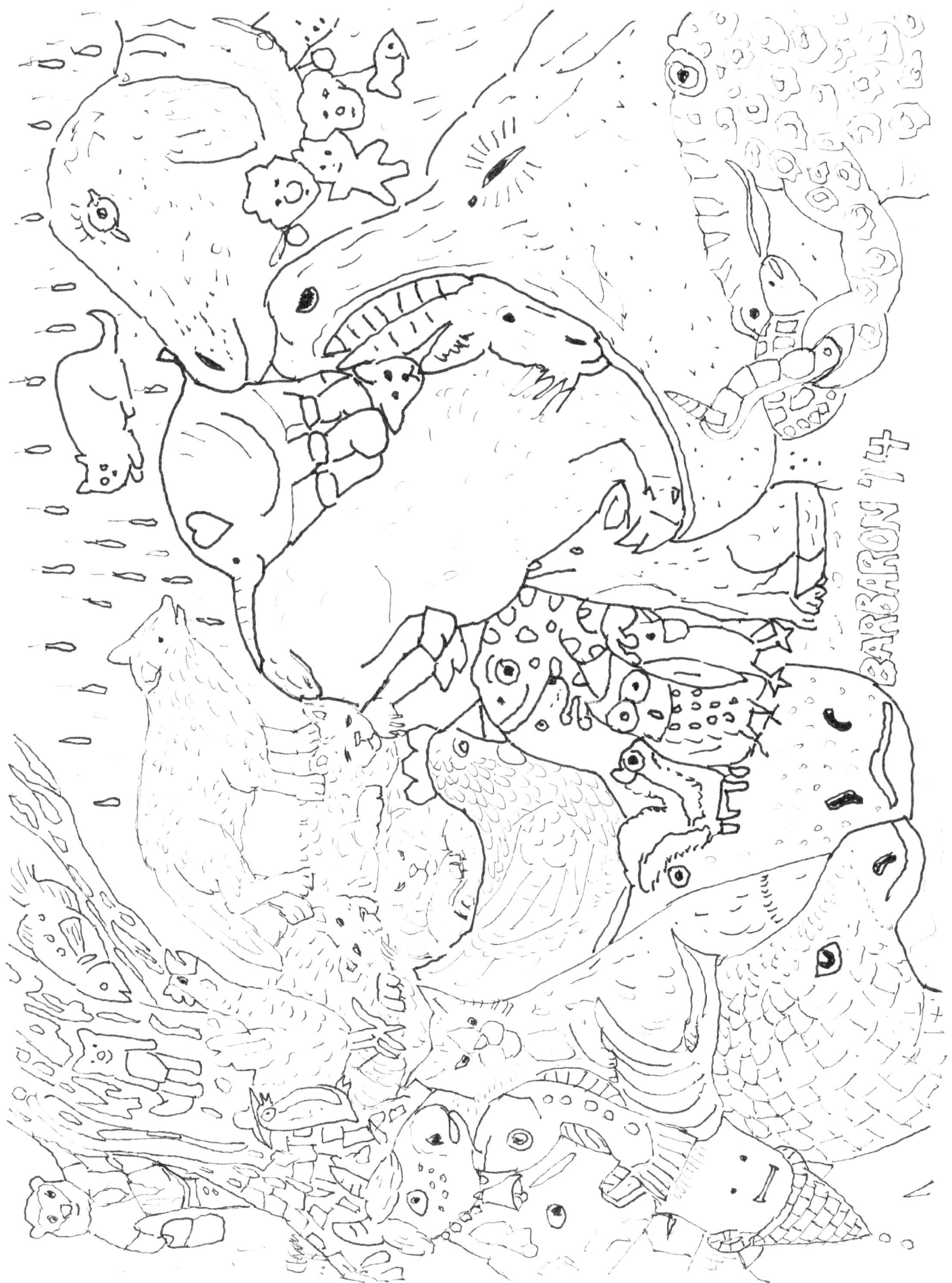

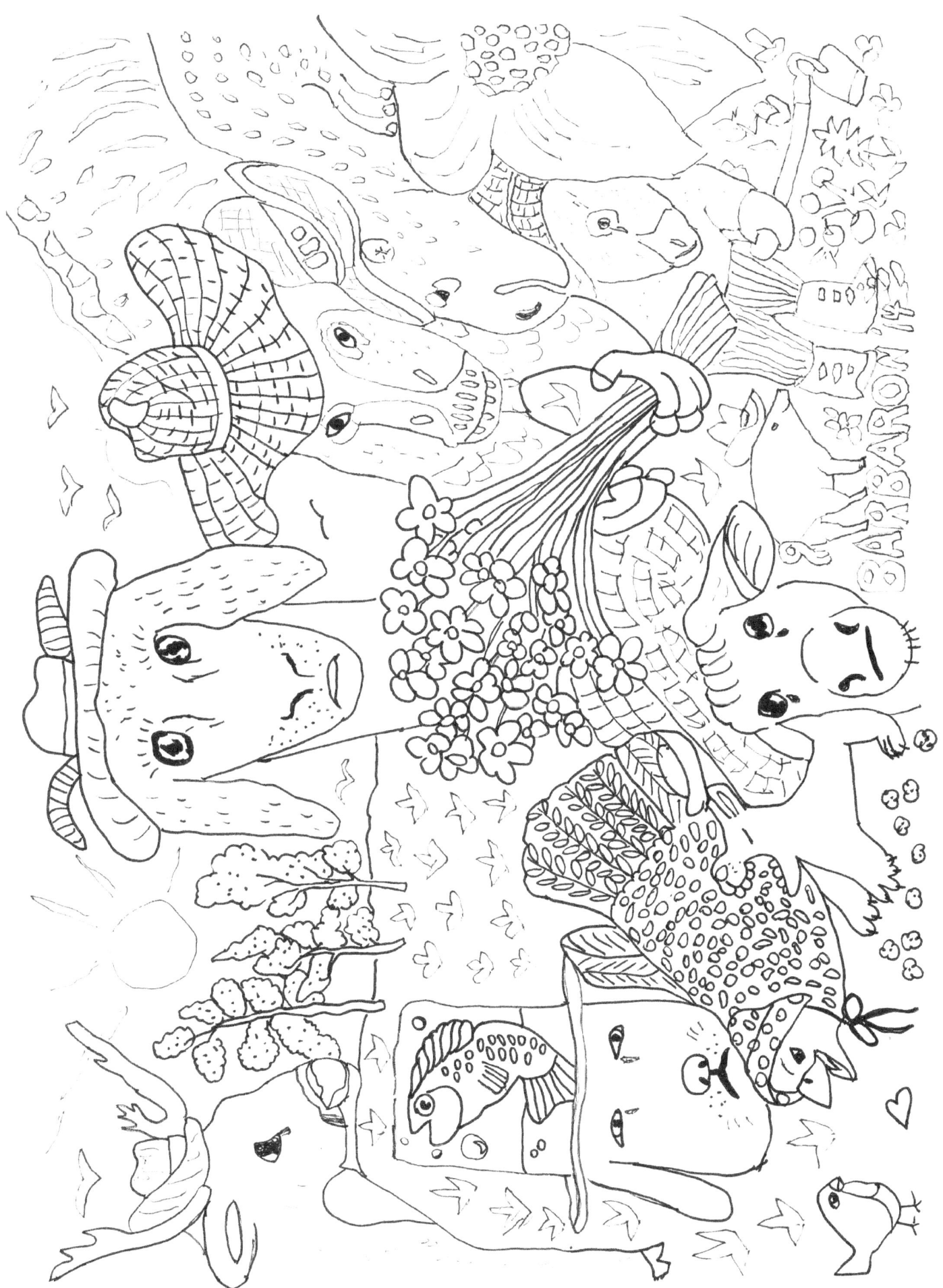

DINA MO GIVES A BOUQUET

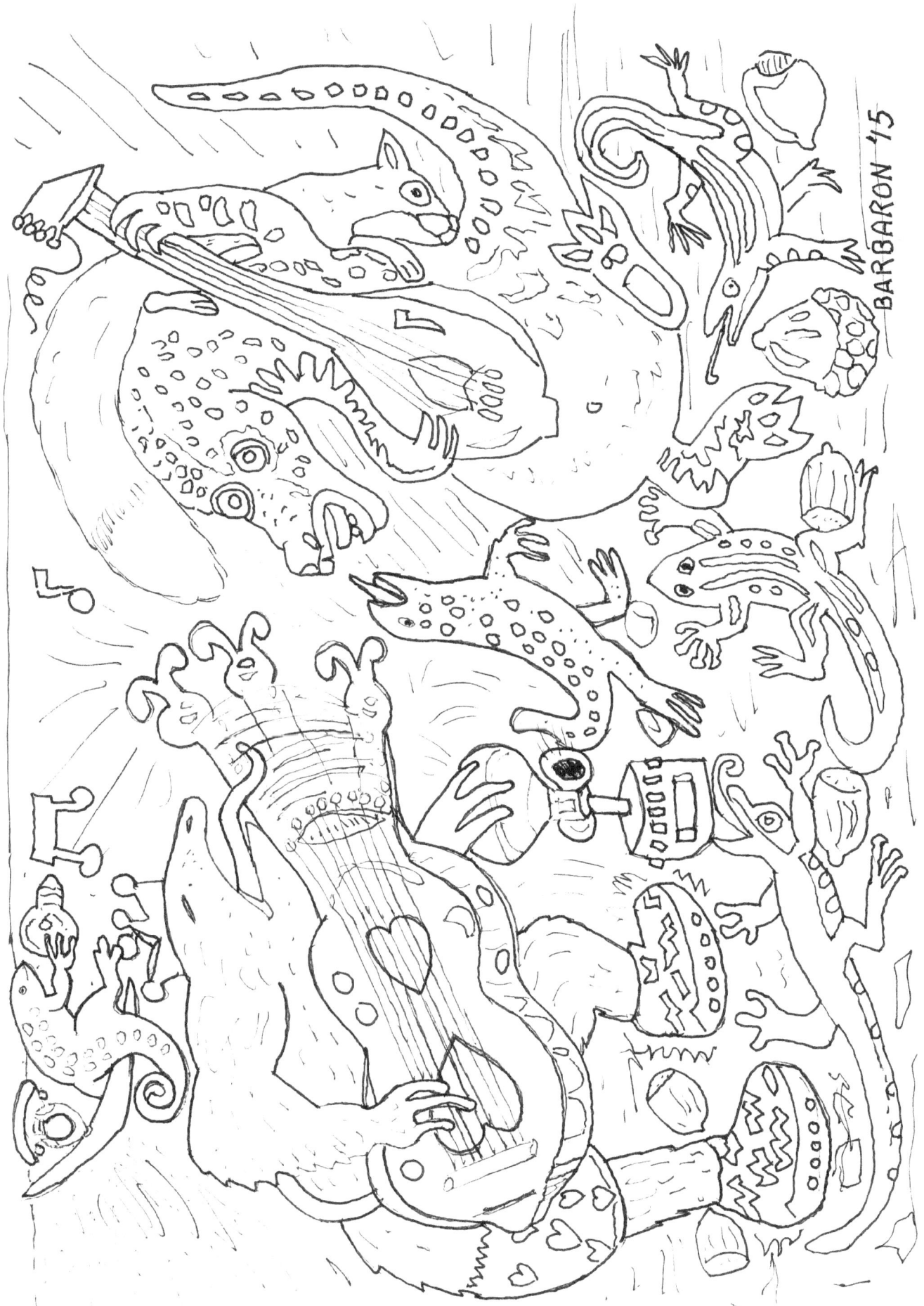

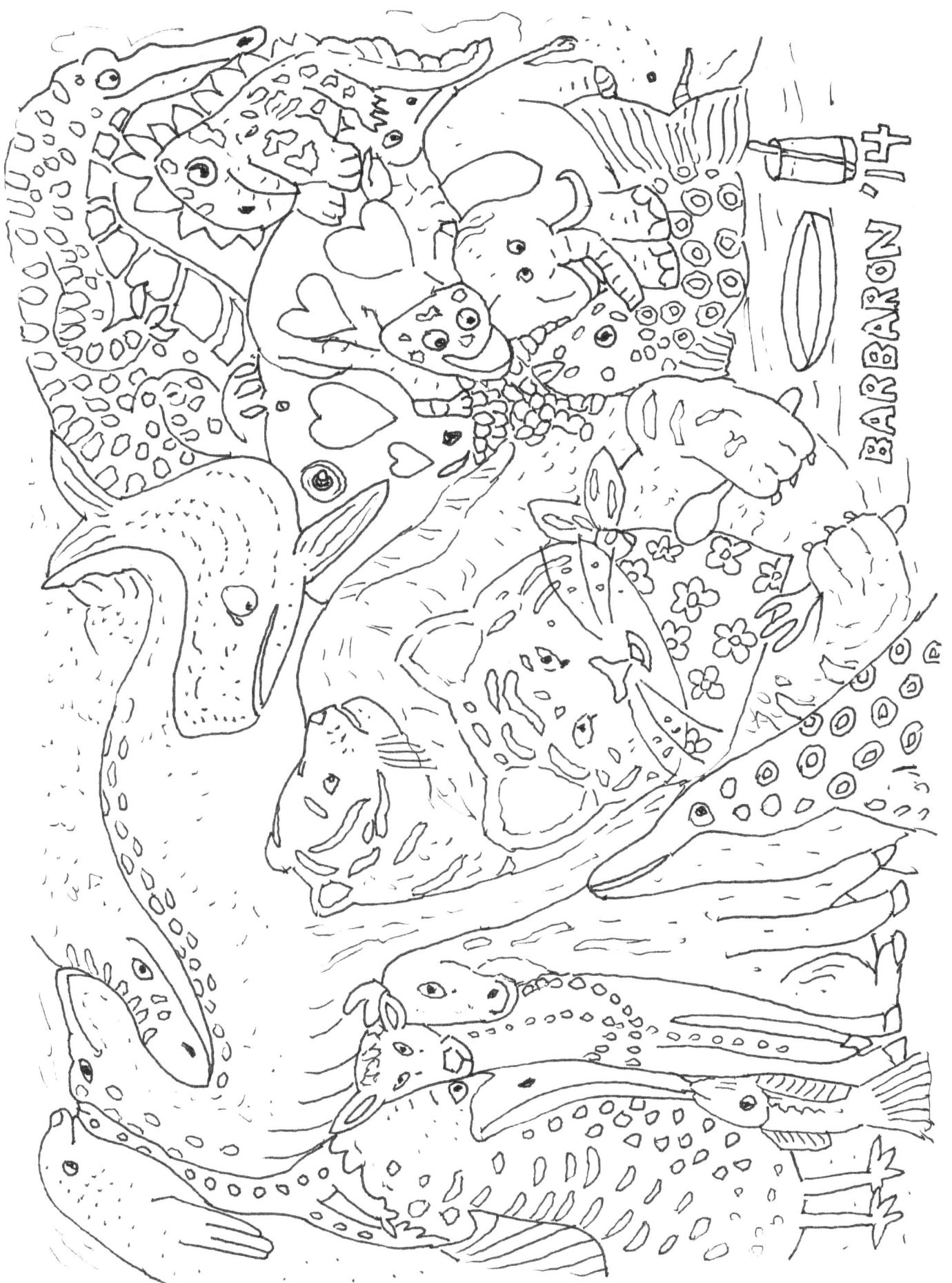

FEED ME

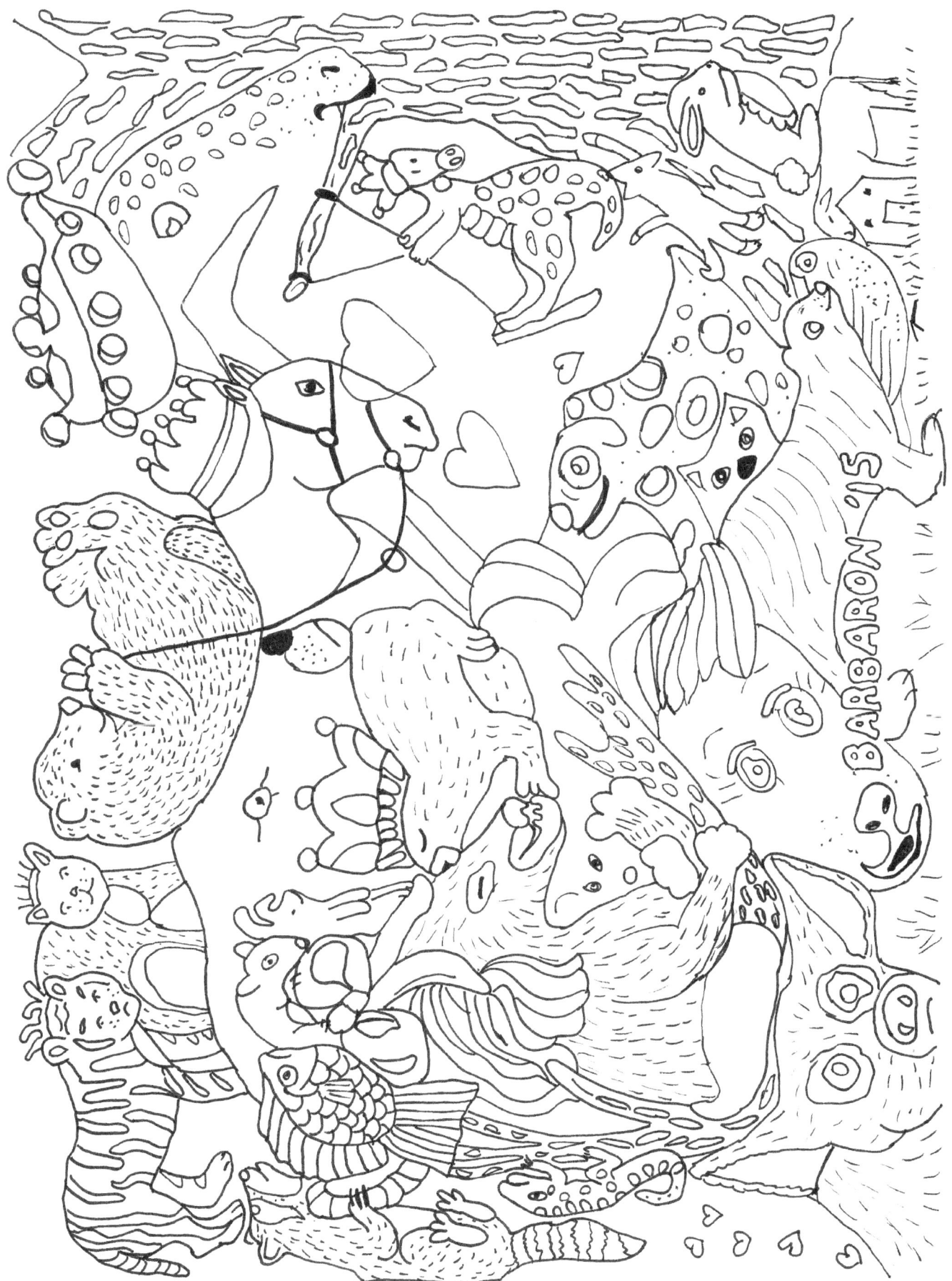

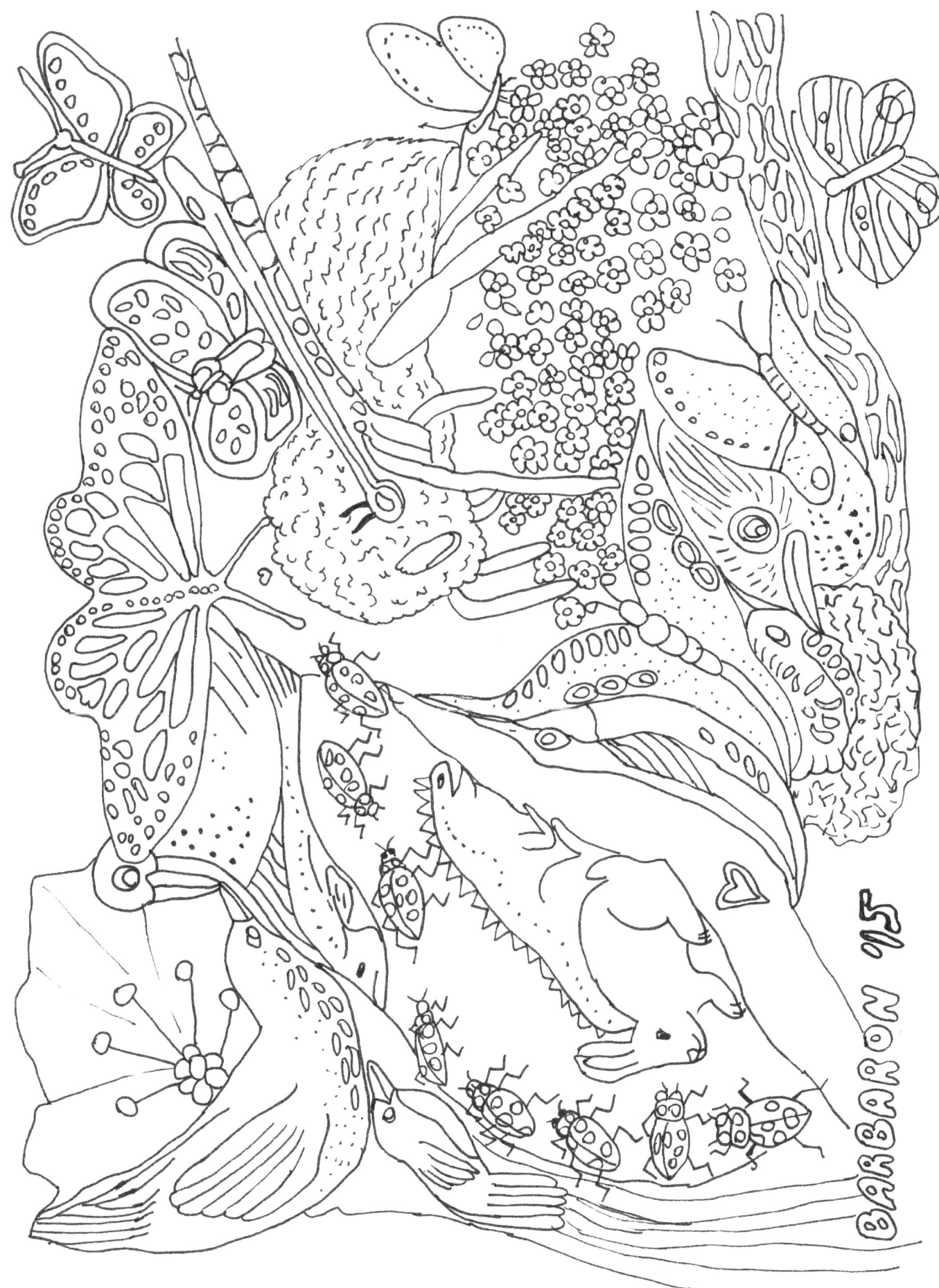

BARBARON '05

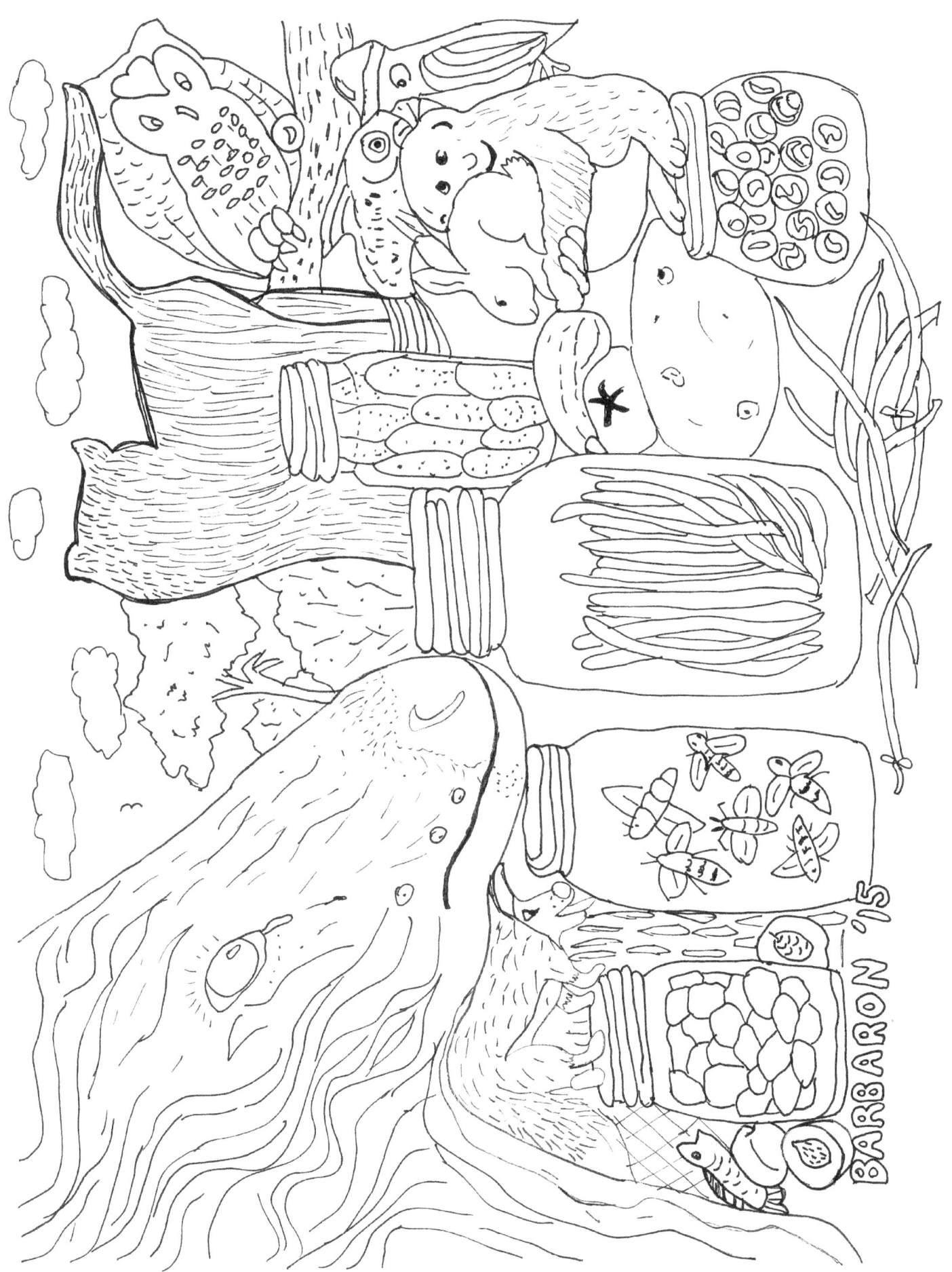

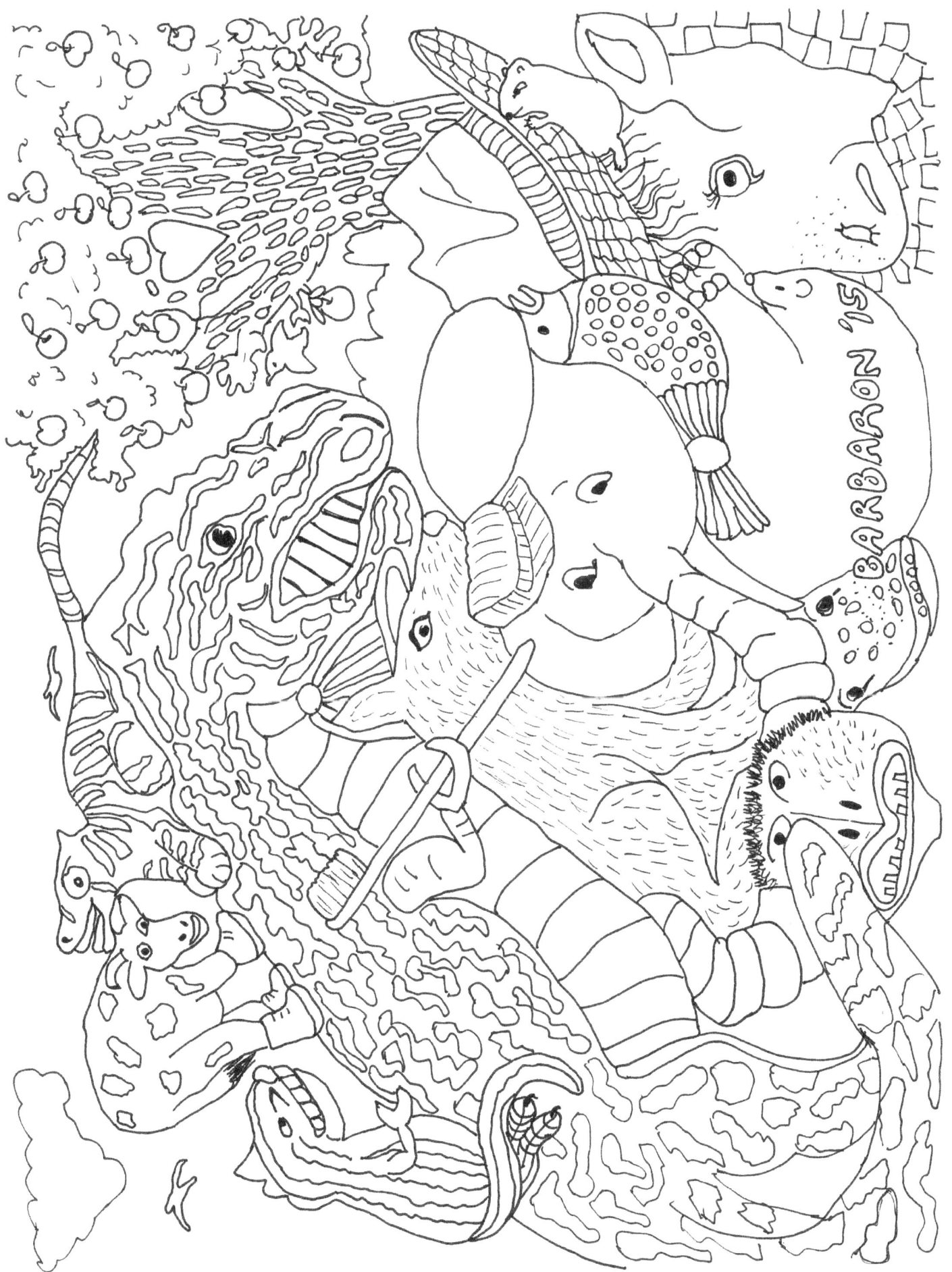

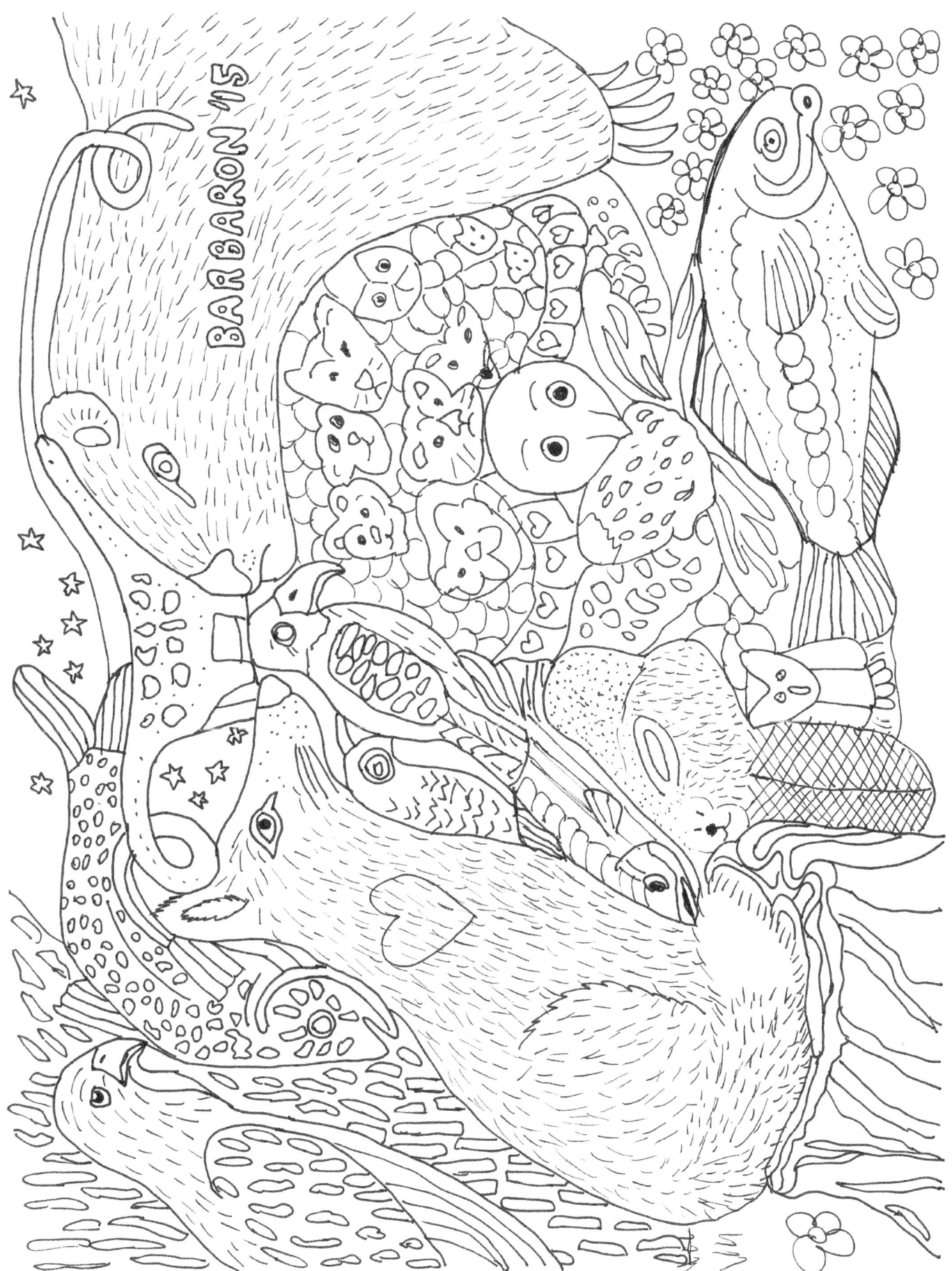

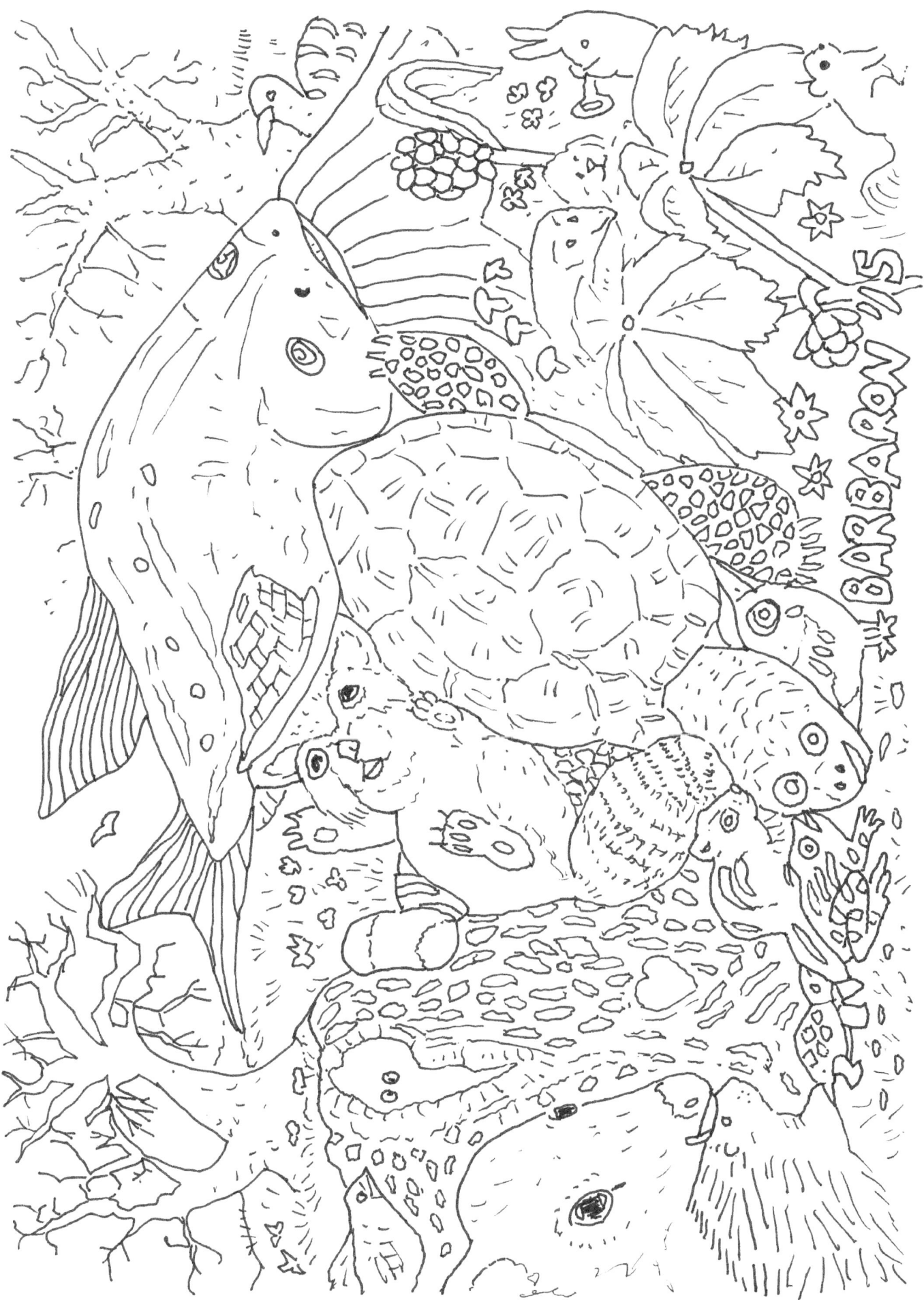

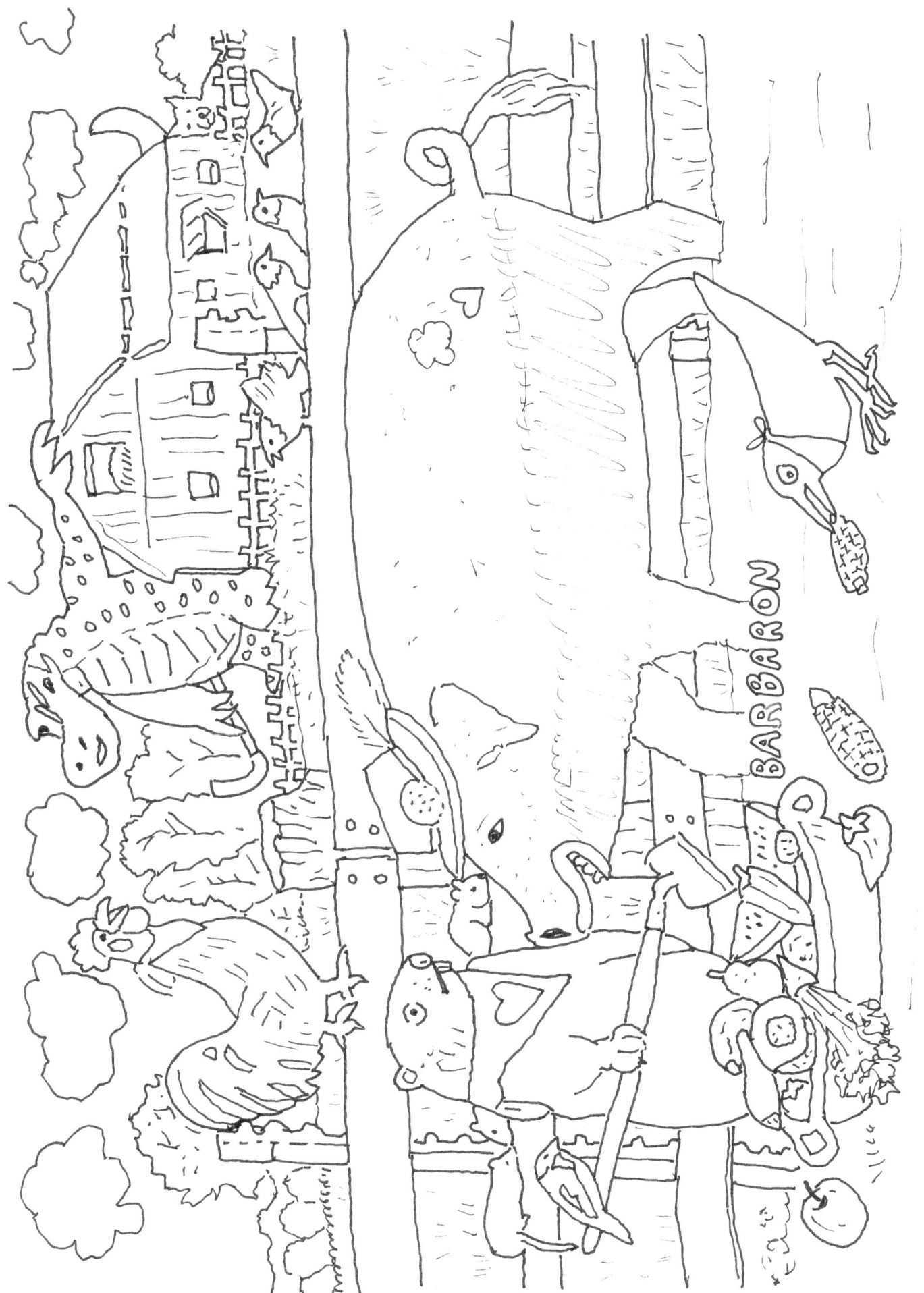

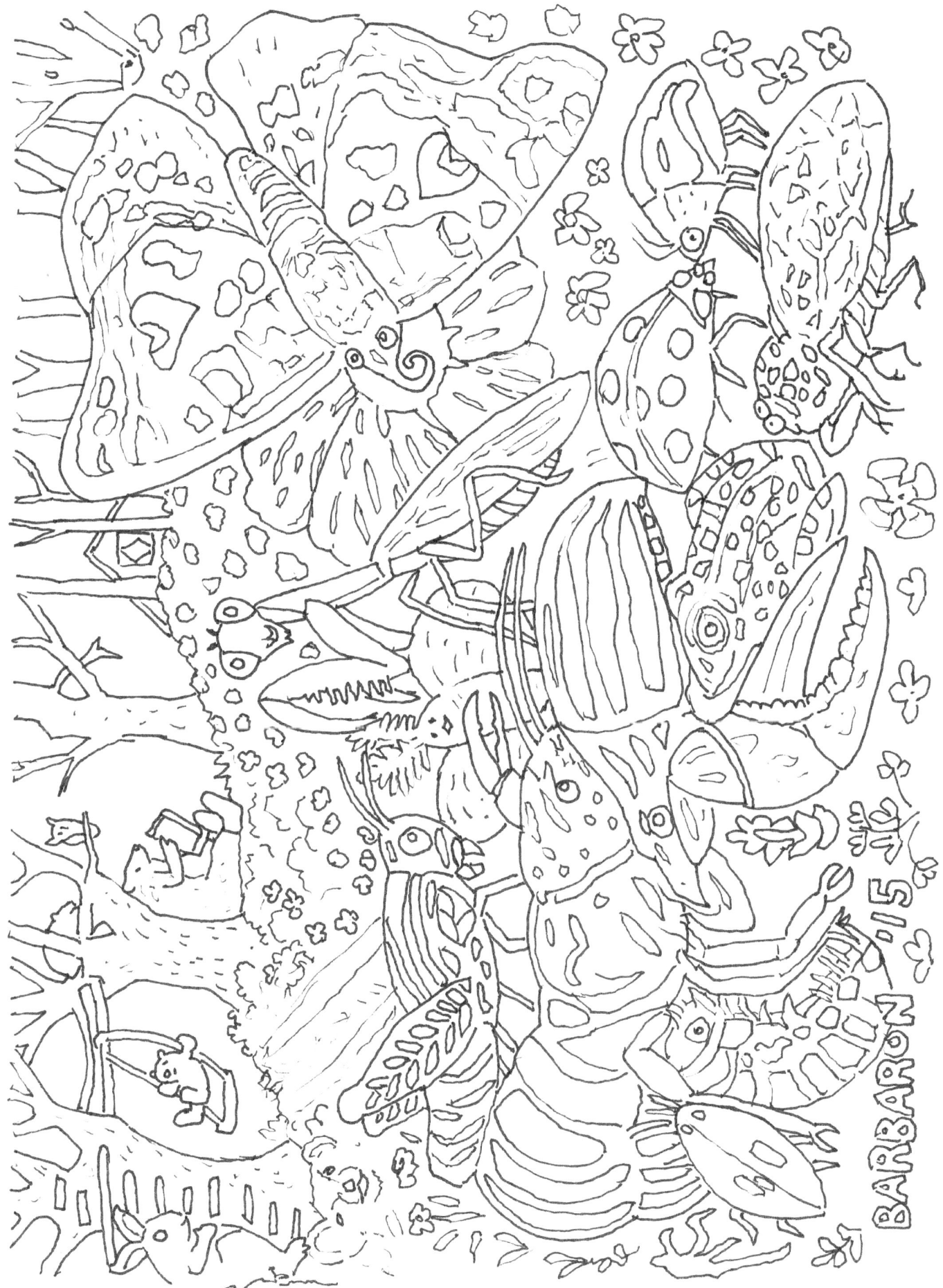

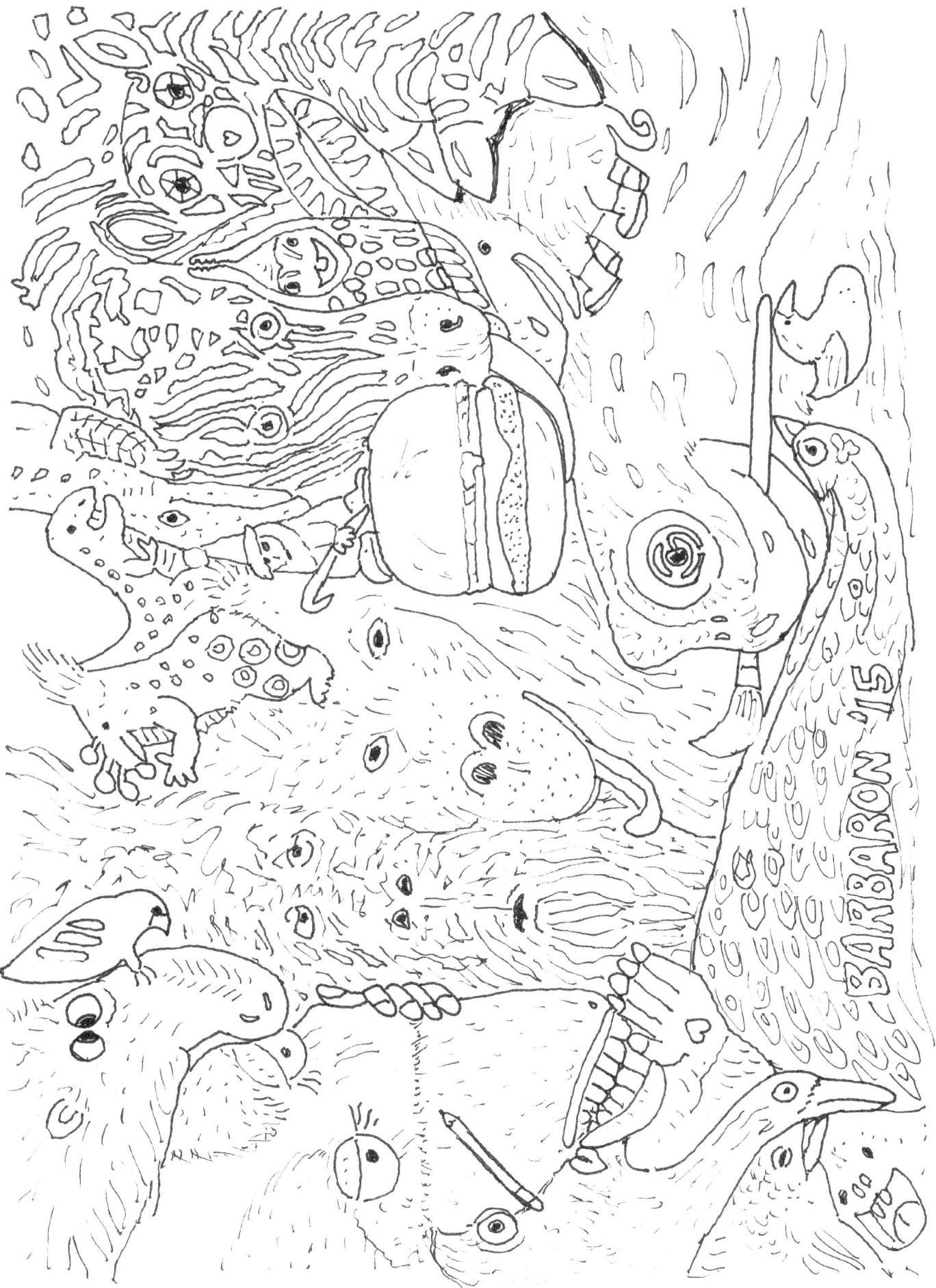

BARBARON '15

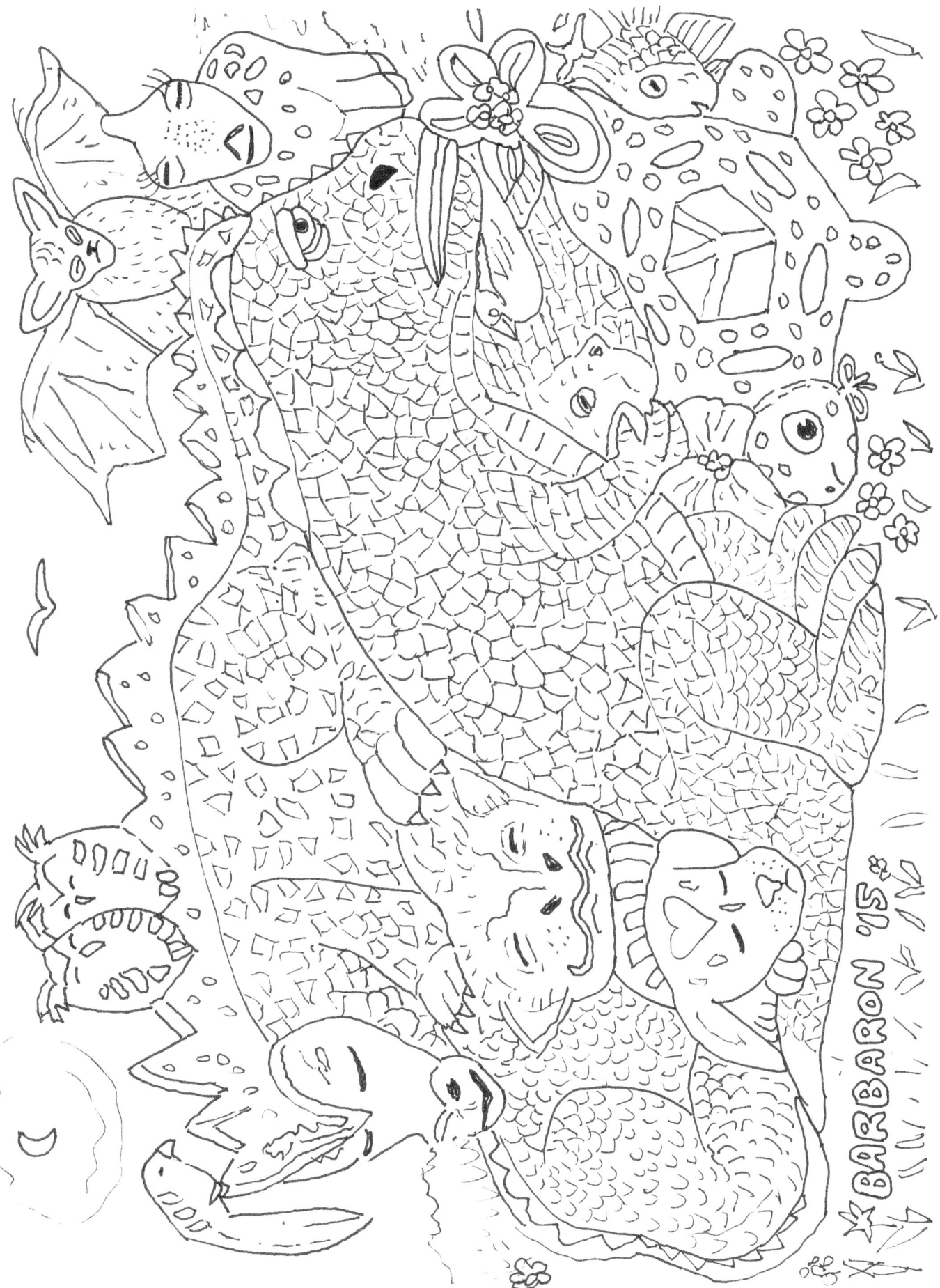

BARBARON '15

BEDTIME FOR DINOSAURS

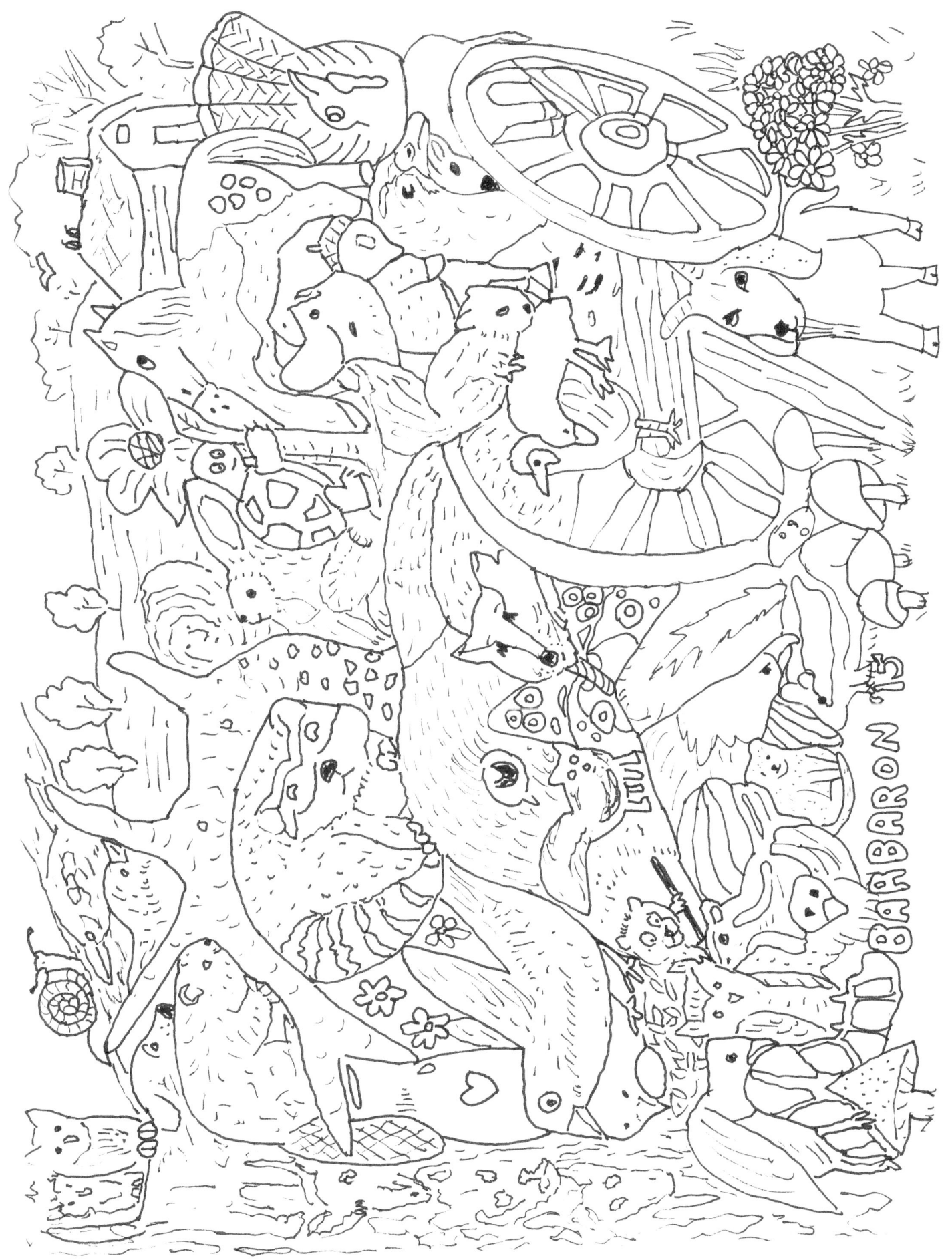

ON THE HILL BEHIND THE BARN

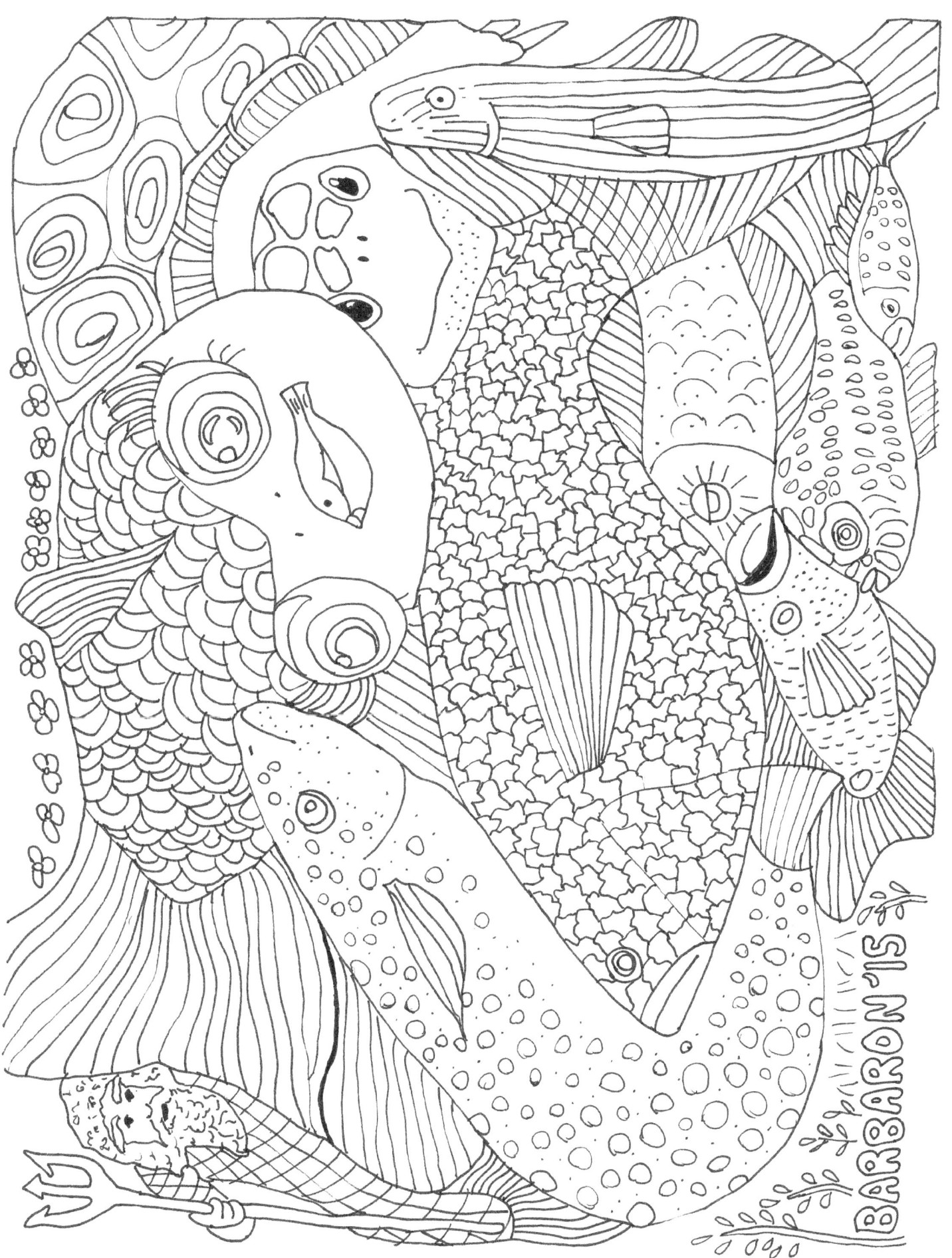

BARBARON '15

PRETTY FISHY

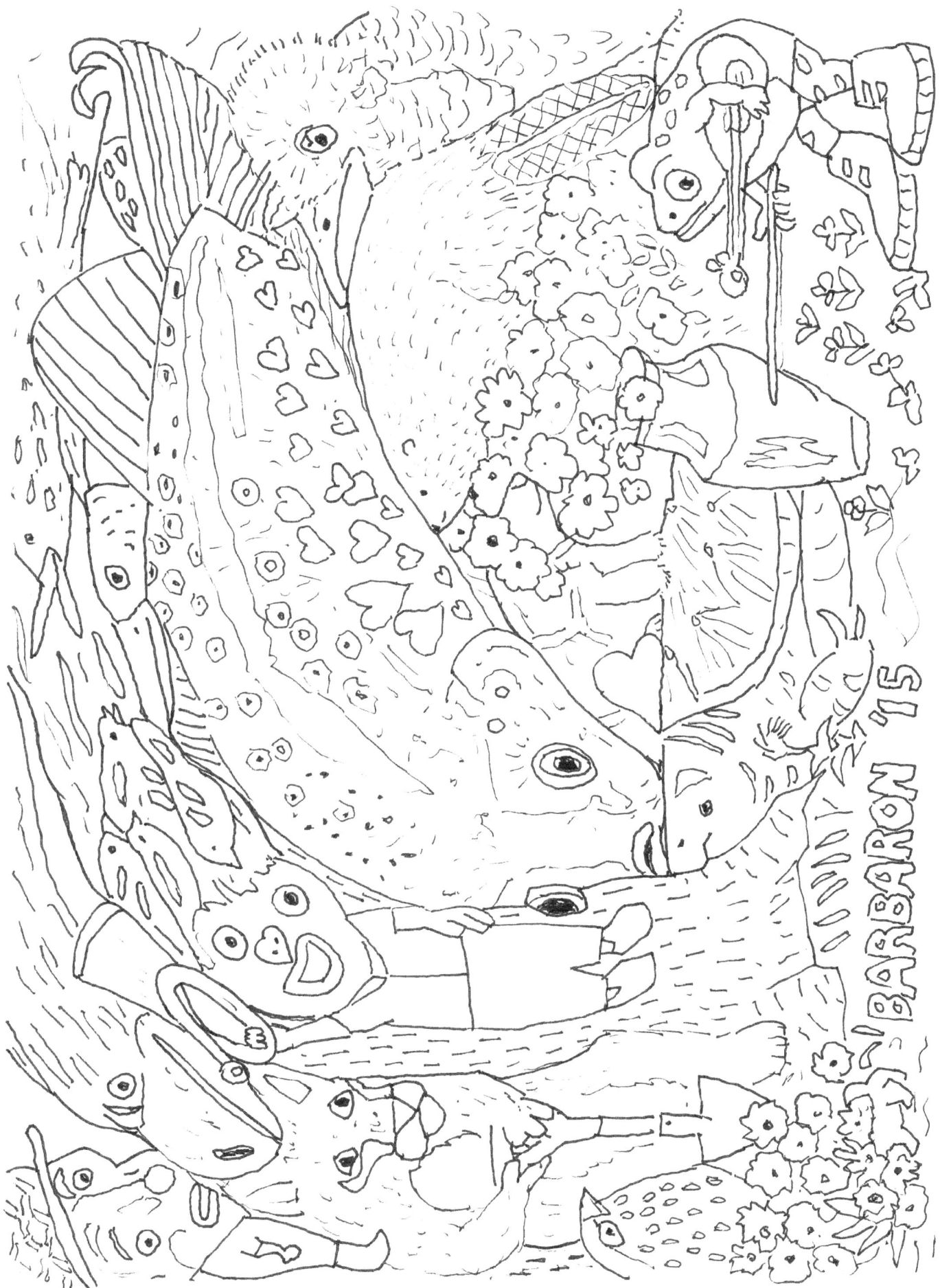

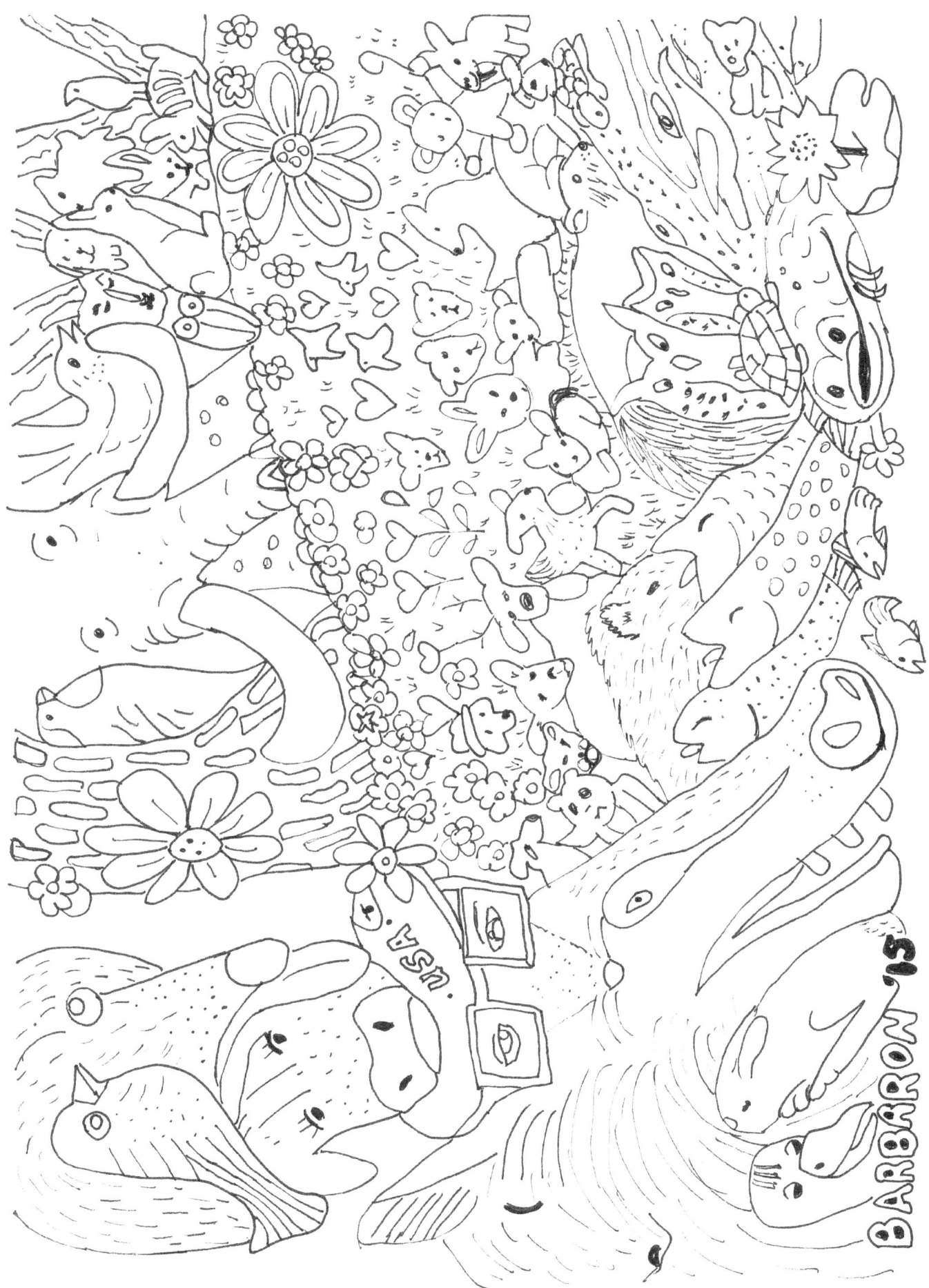

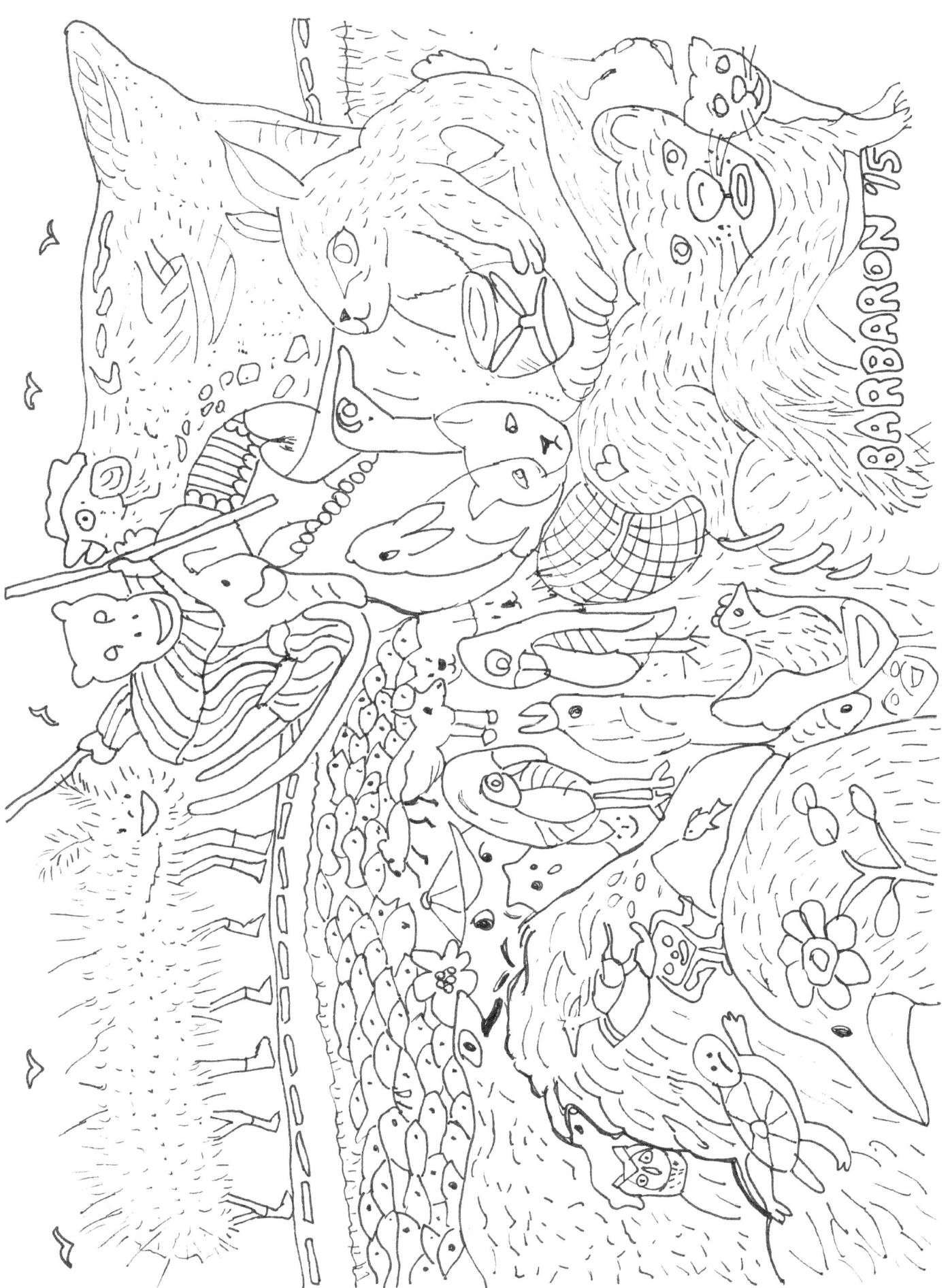

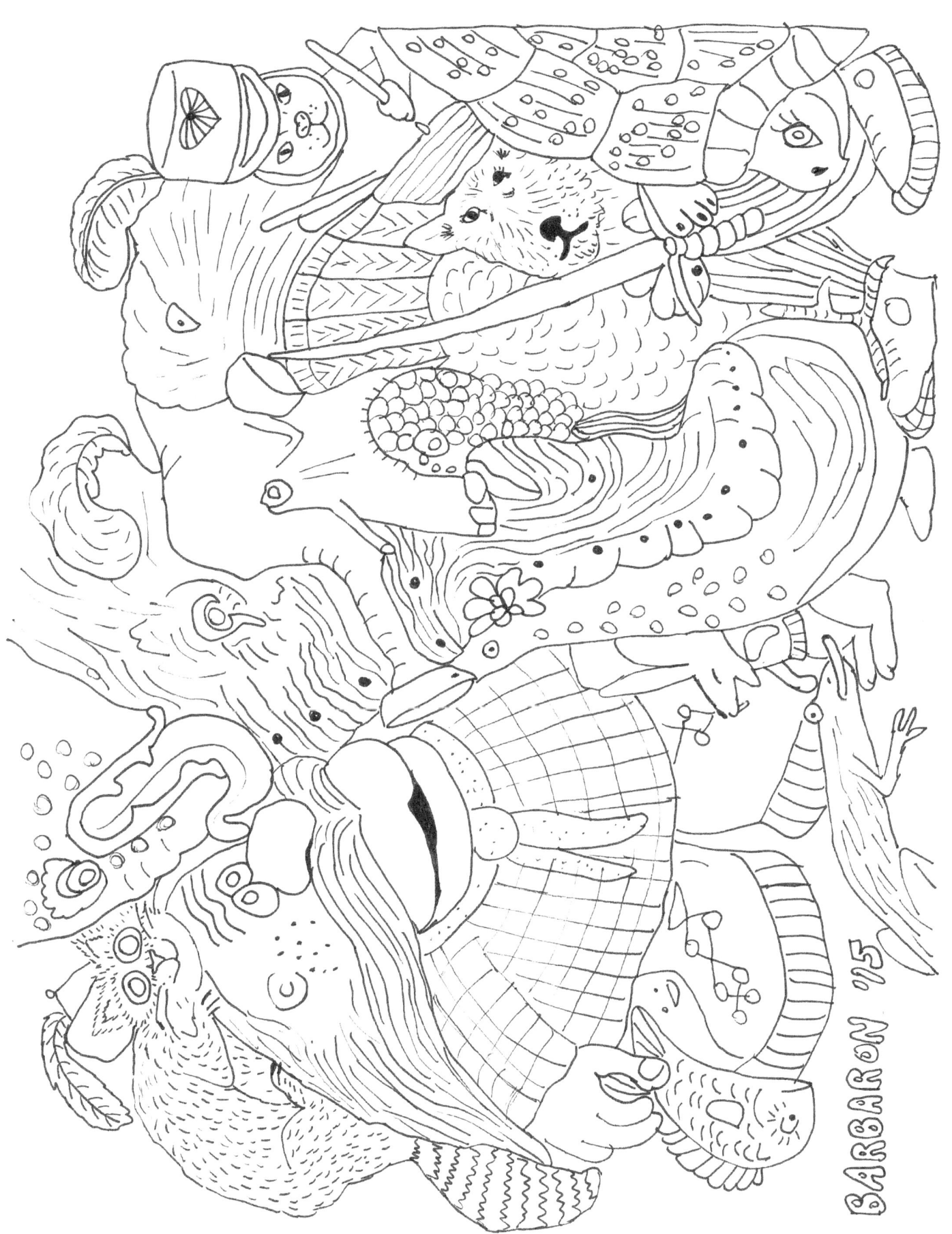

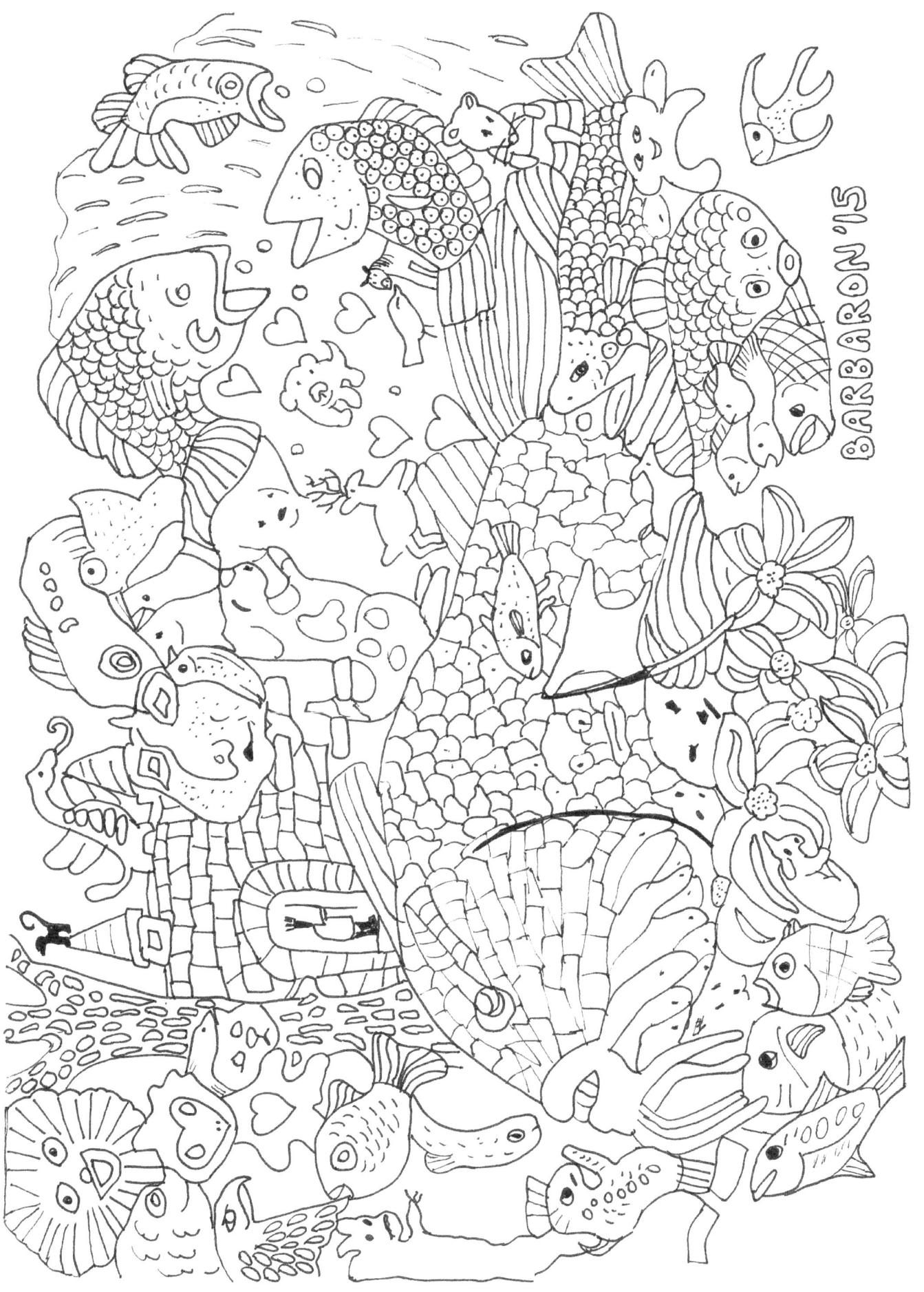

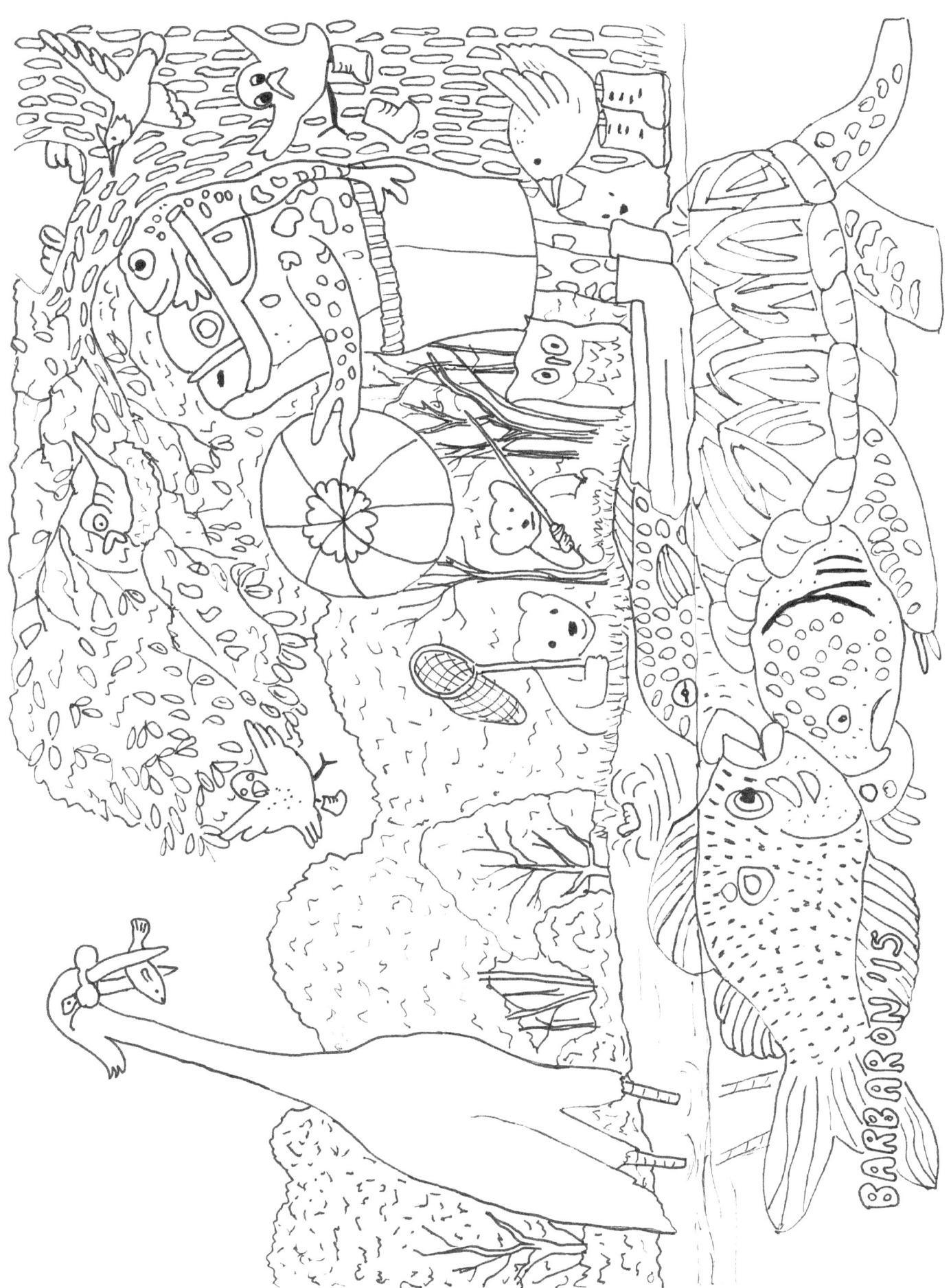

SNORKEL FROG'S SWIMMING LESSON

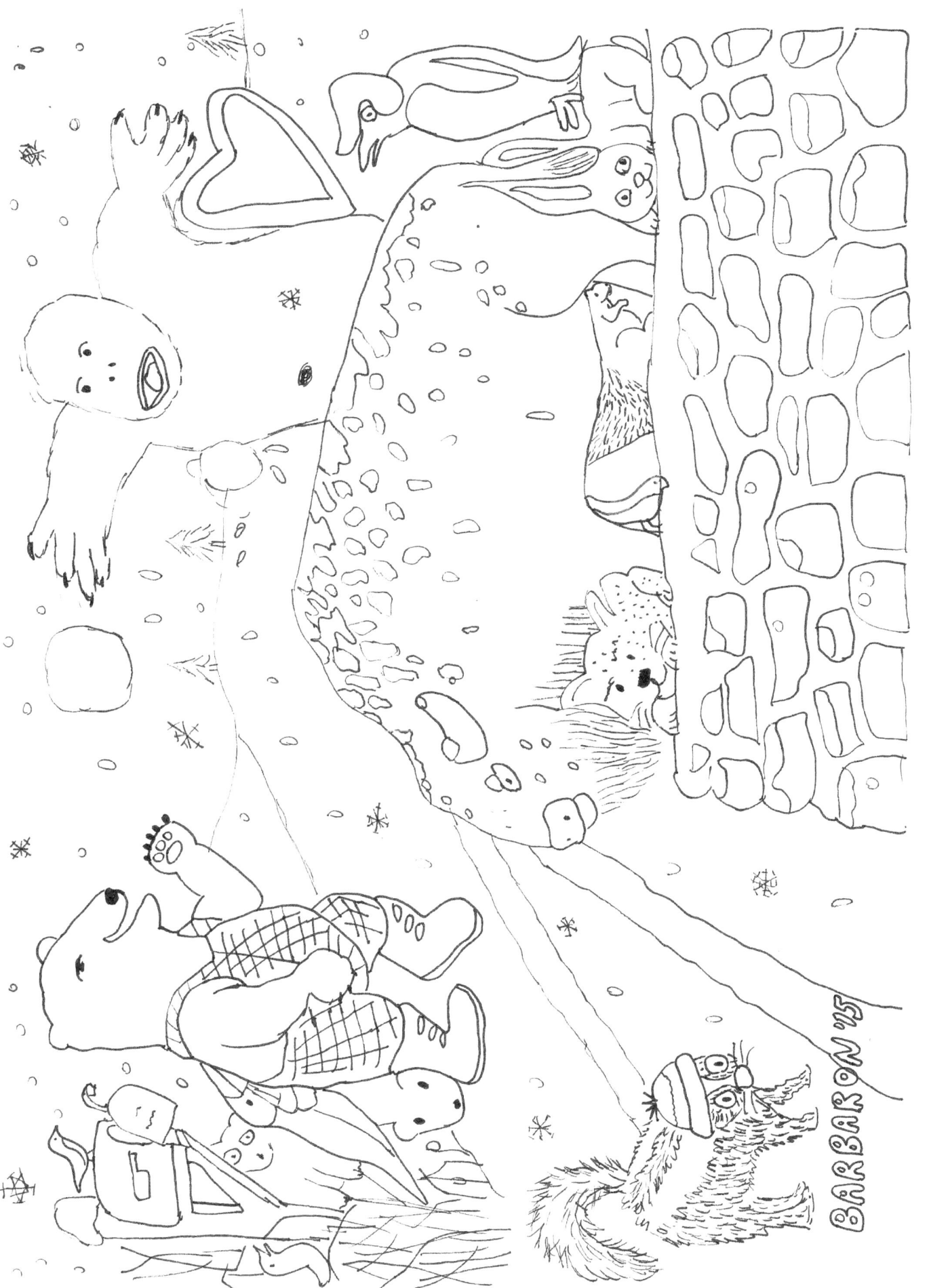

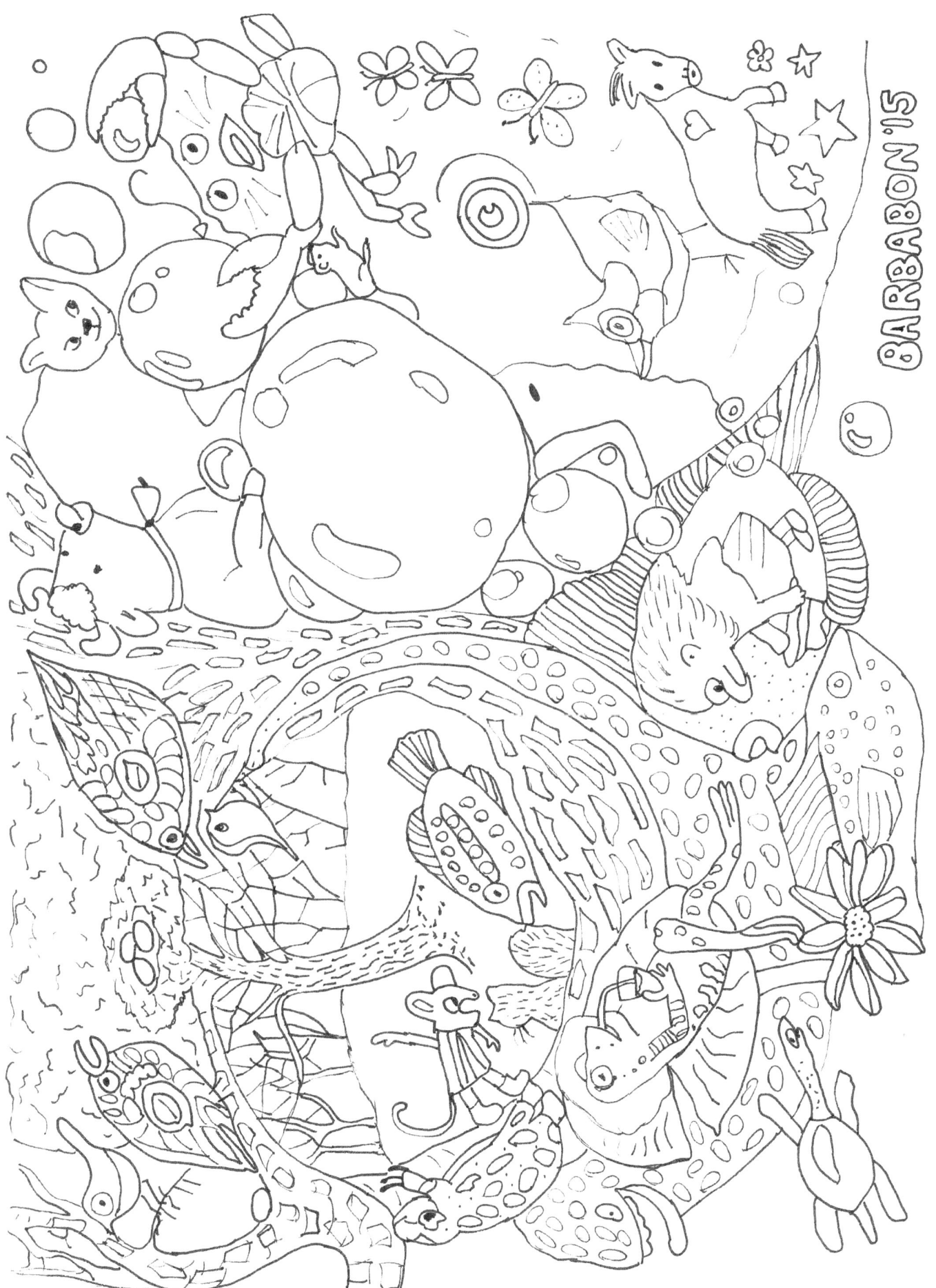

BARBABON '15